If God Loves Me, Why Am I Hurting?

Daniel L. Segraves

If God Loves Me, Why Am I Hurting?

If God Loves Me, Why Am I Hurting?

by Daniel L. Segraves

©Copyright 2010, Daniel L. Segraves
Hazelwood, MO 63042-2299

Cover Design by Laura Jurek

Printed in United States of America.

Printed by

WORD AFLAME PRESS
8855 Dunn Road, Hazelwood, MO 63042
www.pentecostalpublishing.com

Library of Congress Cataloging-in-Publication Data

Segraves, Daniel L., 1946-
  If God loves me, why am I hurting? / Daniel L. Segraves.
      p. cm.
  ISBN 978-1-56722-735-2
  1. Suffering--Religious aspects--United Pentecostal Church
International. 2. Suffering--Biblical teaching. I. Title.
  BV4909.S43 2009
  248.8'6--dc22
                                        2009015192

Contents

Preface

This book has been a long time in the making. Although my wife, Judy, and I had experienced what seemed to us to be a substantial share of suffering, it did not occur to me that a theology of suffering could be discovered in Scripture. I was, of course, aware of the many stories in the Bible about people who suffered and familiar with random verses that discussed the problem, but it was when I took a seminary course, "The Theology of Suffering," that I first began to think of the issue in a holistic way. As a Bible college teacher, I was used to thinking about courses like "Theology of the Church" or "Systematic Theology," but now my eyes were opened to another dimension of theology that could be developed by a careful study of the wide range of biblical evidence on suffering.

In partial fulfillment of the course requirements, I wrote and taught a series of ten lessons for an adult Bible class in 1999. Since the biblical material was very meaningful to me personally and since I knew Judy and I were not the only people who experienced suffering, I also preached and taught on the subject of suffering at a variety of churches and camp meetings. It seemed that everywhere I presented the biblical teaching on suffering it resonated with those who heard it. Many people privately shared their painful experiences with me. It seemed they found it therapeutic to talk with me about their suffering without fear that I would rebuke them for a lack of faith or offer platitudes in response. It became quite clear to me that many people in the church hide their grief and pain because they have discovered that others do not know how to respond in a helpful way.

Then, in 2008, the Media Missions Division of the United Pentecostal Church International asked me to teach a series of lessons to be broadcast on Hope University. I chose the theme "Trusting God in Your Suffering" and wrote and recorded seventeen lessons for broadcast. This book consists of those lessons with slight editing.

I would like to express my appreciation to Norman Paslay II and John Smelser for the opportunity to present these lessons. Both of these men excel in the art of encouragement and affirmation, and it is always a delight to work with them. I am also grateful to Dr. Gregg Allison, who was at that time a professor at Western Seminary, for his excellent work as the teacher for the course "The Theology of Suffering."

I hope this book will help you as you seek to process your pain from a biblical perspective and as you endeavor to minister to others who find themselves in the midst of life's unavoidable suffering.

Introduction

Some years ago at a general conference of the United Pentecostal Church International, I walked with a friend who was several years my elder. As we talked, he asked what my next writing project would be. I told him I was considering writing a book on suffering. His response shocked me.

"What do you know about suffering?" he asked.

Maybe this was his way of inviting me to share with him the suffering Judy and I had experienced to that point. But the way he asked the question seemed to say, "You can't possibly know anything about suffering. How could you write about it?"

But you and I know the truth: Suffering is an inevitable fact of life.

Many years ago, Judy and I made a major move, leaving the church I had pastored for several years and traveling about two thousand miles to a new ministry as a Bible college teacher. The move was especially traumatic for Judy. We loved the people I had pastored, and they loved us. We spent more than seven good years there, and our move was not prompted by any church problems. Instead, I had felt for about two years that God would redirect my ministry into Bible college work. When I received a phone call from the president of the college asking if I had ever considered Bible college work, I took it as God's specific direction. Although we spent twenty-five years in that ministry, I quickly learned that being in God's will does not exempt one from suffering.

Judy's mother and father accompanied us as we traveled across the United States to our new home. The president of the college had also spoken with them about the school's need for a director of food services. Since Judy's parents had previously owned a restaurant and they were looking for a change in life, they accepted this opportunity.

After several days' travel, we arrived at our destination where our first impressions led to culture shock. Our previous life had been in a small community where our children could play outside all day without causing us worry, but our new home was a much larger, culturally diverse city. Although it may not have been the crime capital of the world, as one of our friends who lived there had told us, it did have a very high crime rate in comparison with other cities of equal size. We no longer felt as safe as we had in our previous home. We had to know where our children were at all times.

I'll never forget the knock on our door at about 6:00 AM on the fifth day after our arrival. Judy and I had located a small house to rent and her parents had rented an apartment across town, but things were still chaotic. We had not yet installed telephones; the electricity in our home was not yet turned on; our moving boxes were still packed.

There at the door stood my distraught father-in-law. He said, "I can't get your mother up!" We jumped into our cars and raced to their apartment. We arrived to discover Judy's mother had died during the night. It was later determined she had passed away at about 2:00 AM that morning from heart failure. She was fifty-three years old.

At her mother's funeral, some of the good-intentioned people we had just met said to Judy, "You are so strong!" They were wrong. Judy was not strong. She was in shock. Many were the nights during that first year that I held her as she trembled, shaking from fears known and unknown.

During that year, the trauma associated with my mother-in-law's death intensified because the Bible school was in such financial straits, my paycheck was regularly six weeks—and sometimes as much as two months—late. Judy and I had saved a few thousand dollars before our move, hoping to buy a house in the small town where I had pastored. We used up that money during the first year in our new home. We needed it just to survive.

I will not attempt to recount all of the events that introduced us to the reality of suffering. I will just say we know, as you do, that suffering is part of life. You cannot avoid suffering by being in the will of God. You cannot elude it with positive confessions. Prayer, fasting, or any other spiritual discipline cannot detour around it. Neither will it help to knock on wood, avoid crossing the path of a black cat, or refusing to open an umbrella indoors!

The word most often used to summarize the problem of suffering for people who believe in God is theodicy. A technical term for the defense of God, theodicy is composed from two Greek words, theos (God) and dikē (justice). The word theodicy is used to capture the idea of showing God to be just or right. A common question is, if there is a God, and if He is a good God who is omnipotent (all powerful), omniscient (all knowing), and loving, why does He allow suffering? That is the question we will explore in this book.

1

Is There Any Hope?

E ach new report of school or workplace shootings, domestic violence, ethnic cleansing, or terrorist brutality forcibly reminds us that we live in a horribly broken world. Americans will never forget the first inconceivable reports of September 11, 2001. Although it was not the first event of its kind, the tragedy at Columbine High School in Littleton, Colorado, struck terror in the human heart; this was not how things should be. When we hear this kind of bad news, we may at first react with disbelief, fear, and anger. But soon, because we are solution-oriented people, we start asking, "What went wrong here? What can we do to 'fix' this problem so it won't happen again?"

We look for scapegoats. First we blame the perpetrators of the violence. Then we tend to blame their families and specifically their parents. We blame those who are said to have "provoked" the violence. We may blame the school system, the teachers, and the administrators. We widen the spectrum of blame to gun manufacturers, weapons dealers, and the government for failing to adequately regulate the sale of firearms. In our culture, we also pinpoint the influence of violent television programs, movies, video games, and Internet sites that promote violent behavior. We even blame the various religions of the world for international conflict. When politics enters the picture, it is not uncommon to hear the blame pinned on faulty foreign policy. Then there are those who embrace various conspiracy theories and insist that suffering and death are orchestrated by the manipulations of the elite of society, either for monetary or political gain.

It is certainly right to do whatever can be done to minimize wrong influences, to promote wholesome influences, and to protect people from violence, abuse, and manipulation. Soon after the tragedy at Columbine, the school district in Vancouver, Washington, required students to tote transparent backpacks. Guards checked the identification of every person coming on campus to assure they were students. After years of political disagreement on the subject, Democrat and Republican senators introduced enhanced gun control. Then a Republican presidential candidate spoke out in favor of increased gun control. The President of the United States of America urged parents to limit access to television programming for their children, and he called on the producers of movies in Hollywood to weed the violence out of their productions.

We Are Broken People Living in a Broken World

We should applaud every effort to limit evil and never resign ourselves to the proliferation of wickedness. Whatever can be done to promote a safer environment must be done, including legislation, greater restraint in the media and entertainment, economic justice, family renewal, and international diplomacy.

Above all, the church must more aggressively declare the gospel message of hope and renewal. This message does not merely seek to minimize violence; it results in human transformation and provides an inner check on destructive behavior.

In the final analysis, however, there will never be peace on this earth until the Prince of Peace, Jesus Christ, returns to rule the nations with a "rod of iron." The prophet David recorded the following profound words of the coming Messiah.

I will declare the decree: The Lord has said to Me, "You are My Son, today I have begotten You. Ask of Me, and I will give You the nations for Your inheritance, and the ends of the earth for Your possession. You shall break them with a rod of iron; You shall dash them to pieces like a potter's vessel" (Psalm 2:7-9).

This prophetic statement, portions of which are quoted ten times in the New Testament, will be fulfilled at the second coming of Jesus, which the apostle John saw in a startling vision. John saw the heavens opened and one called Faithful and True riding out on a white horse, accompanied by the armies of Heaven. This rider's name was "The Word of God," and His robe and thigh bore the words, "KING OF KINGS AND LORD OF LORDS." Drawing from David's prophecy, John wrote, "Now out of His mouth [went] a sharp sword, that with it He should strike the nations. And He Himself will rule them with a rod of iron" (Revelation 19:15a). The ancient prophet Isaiah anticipated the nature of His rule when he penned the following words.

For unto us a Child is born, unto us a Son is given; and the government will be upon His shoulder. And His name will be called Wonderful, Counselor, Mighty God, Everlasting Father, Prince of Peace. Of the increase of His government and peace there will be no end, upon the throne of David and over His kingdom, to order it and establish it with judgment and justice from that time forward, even forever. The zeal of the Lord of hosts will perform this (Isaiah 9:6-7).

In His first coming, Jesus Christ brought redemption from sin for those who believe on Him and embrace the good news, the gospel. This restores fellowship with God and peace in the human heart. In His second coming, our Lord and Savior will also bring peace to the planet. Immediately after John saw Jesus returning on a white horse to exercise His authority over the nations of the earth, he saw Satan being bound and cast into a bottomless pit for one thousand years, banned from deceiving the nations. Christ will govern the whole earth, sharing His reign with those who believe on Him. True peace will reign on earth as well as in the human heart.

The apostle John, who wrote the Book of Revelation near the end of the first century, was not the only one to tell of this coming day of universal peace. The Hebrew prophets also anticipated it. Isaiah wrote an extended description of the characteristics of the Messiah's rule.

His delight is in the fear of the Lord, and He shall not judge by the sight of His eyes, nor decide by the hearing of His ears; but with righteousness He shall judge the poor, and decide with equity for the meek of the earth; He shall strike the earth with the rod of His mouth, and with the breath of His lips He shall slay the wicked. Righteousness shall be the belt of His loins, and faithfulness the belt of His waist. The wolf also shall dwell with the lamb, the leopard shall lie down with the young goat, the calf and the young lion and the fatling together; and a little child shall lead them. The cow and the bear shall graze; their young ones shall lie down together; and the lion shall eat straw like the ox. The nursing child shall play by the cobra's hole, and the weaned child shall put his hand in the viper's den. They shall not hurt nor destroy in all My holy mountain, for the earth shall be full of the knowledge of the Lord as the waters cover the sea (Isaiah 11:3-9).

This ancient prophecy shares a definite link with John's vision. Both Isaiah and John said the Messiah would judge with righteousness. Isaiah said the belt of the Messiah's waist was faithfulness; John wrote the Messiah was faithful and true. Isaiah declared the Messiah would strike the earth with the rod of His mouth; John said a sharp sword would go out of the Messiah's mouth with which He would strike the nations, ruling them with a rod of iron.

All of this sounds wonderful. And, like the prophecies about the first coming of the Messiah, these will one day be fulfilled. Unfortunately, these future references do not bring order to the present chaos. As we wait for the day when peace will reign on this earth, we face the reality of brokenness.

Today, our merely human judges make decisions based only on what they see and hear. As a result, justice is sometimes not done. Far too often, the innocent languish in prison.

Today, the poor are often oppressed, ignored, abused.

Today, aggressors in positions of power and influence often trample over the meek.

Today, the wolf is not dwelling peacefully with the lamb, the righteous are not reigning on the earth, little children are often the most abused and wounded, and the earth is not yet full of the knowledge of the Lord.

We have not yet beaten our swords into plowshares and our spears into pruning hooks.[1] Conflicts continually agitate between nations, and war is at the top of the planet's curriculum.

Satan is not yet cast into the bottomless pit. His frenzy of deceiving the nations will continue until the heavens open to reveal that awesome rider on a white horse whose eyes are like a flame of fire and on whose head are many crowns.

Until that day, the words of the apostle Paul still apply.

But know this, that in the last days perilous times will come: For men will be lovers of themselves, lovers of money, boasters, proud, blasphemers, disobedient to parents, unthankful, unholy, unloving, unforgiving, slanderers, without self-control, brutal, despisers of good, traitors, headstrong, haughty, lovers of pleasure rather than lovers of God, having a form of godliness but denying its power (II Timothy 3:1-5a).

In a continuing discussion of life as it will be until the end, Paul further declared, "Yes, and all who desire to live godly in Christ Jesus will suffer persecution. But evil men and imposters will grow worse and worse, deceiving and being deceived" (II Timothy 3:12-13).

Paul's negative characterizations of people in the last days is depressing. We would rather not hear them. No one is encouraged or uplifted by the idea of living among self-centered, greedy, arrogant, blaspheming rebels who have no gratitude for any good thing and whose lifestyle is devoid of all that is holy. Who wants to associate with loveless, bitter, brutal slanderers who cannot control themselves and who despise everything good? How can we befriend headstrong, haughty traitors whose chief ambition in life is to wallow in every sensual pleasure? And what are we to think of those whose lives contain any assortment of these foul traits but who profess religions that endorse and even encourage such behavior?

I agree. These are depressing and discouraging words. Perhaps Paul would not be welcome in many of today's pulpits.

But wait. As much as we would like to deny the reality of pain, suffering, and evil all around us, many of us are quite familiar with the fear that springs unbidden when the telephone rings in the darkest hours of the night. We know about the quickened pulse and wildly racing imagination upon seeing a uniformed person standing at our door. We dread the somber countenance of the medical doctor approaching us from the surgery room.

The reason things will get worse and not better is that we are broken people living in a broken world.

God never intended for the world to writhe in pain, suffering, and violence as it does today. He created human beings in His own image[2] and delegated to them authority over the earth, including the responsibility and ability to "subdue" it.[3] He placed Adam and Eve in a paradise, free from fear, shame, violence, sickness, suffering, poverty, and dysfunctional relationships. But that idyllic existence was not to endure.

Whence Brokenness?

Adam and Eve's rebellion against God—with all of its consequences—introduced sin into the world. There was "trouble in Paradise." The first result of sin was shame and guilt, sensations unknown to Adam and Eve before their sin.[4] After they ate the fruit of the forbidden tree, they tried to fix their problem themselves in a vain attempt to cover up the consequences of their rebellion against God. Blame and fear fractured their relationship as Adam rejected his personal responsibility and blamed his wife directly and God indirectly for his sin.[5] God asked Adam, "Have you eaten from the tree of which I commanded you that you should not eat?" (Genesis 3:11). Adam answered, "The woman whom You gave to be with me, she gave me of the tree, and I ate" (Genesis 3:12). Turning to Eve, the Lord God asked, "What is this you have done?" (Genesis 3:13). Eve also attempted to evade personal responsibility. She said, "The serpent deceived me, and I ate." (See Genesis 3:13.)

Before God created Eve, He had warned Adam not to eat of the tree of the knowledge of good and evil. He said, "In the day that you eat of it you shall surely die" (Genesis 2:17). The Scripture always presents death as some kind of separation. Physical death occurs when the material and immaterial parts of human existence are separated. Spiritual death occurs when people are separated from fellowship with God. Paul wrote that before we were made alive in Christ, we "were dead in trespasses and sins" (Ephesians 2:1).

Just as God had warned, Adam and Eve experienced death—separation from fellowship with God—as a consequence of their sin. Other consequences included the divine curse on the serpent,[6] physical pain for Eve, relational tension between spouses,[7] and the removal of human ability to subdue the earth as indicated by a curse on the ground.[8]

Not the least of the consequences of sin was that Adam and Eve were driven from Paradise, barred from the Tree of Life, and thrust—in a sense "homeless"—into the world.[9]

Apparently not long afterward, as Adam and Eve and their two sons struggled for existence in this strange, foreign world, Cain perpetrated the first act of violence. He "was very angry, and his countenance fell" because God accepted Abel's offering and not his own. "So the Lord said to Cain, 'Why are you angry? And why has your countenance fallen? If you do well, will you not be accepted? And if you do not do well, sin lies at the door. And its desire is for you, but you should rule over it'" (Genesis 4:5-7). Anger. Dejection. How early these destructive emotions surfaced in the fallen world! Rather than responding in a positive way to God's invitation to do the right thing, "Cain talked with Abel his brother; and it came to pass, when they were in the field, that Cain rose up against Abel his brother and killed him" (Genesis 4:8). The ensuing proliferation of violence is seen in Lamech's boast, the earliest poem in the Bible. Lamech said to his wives, "Adah and Zillah, hear my voice; wives of Lamech, listen to my speech! For I have killed a man for wounding me, even a young man for hurting me. If Cain shall be avenged sevenfold, then Lamech seventy-sevenfold" (Genesis 4:23-24). The day came when the human race was so thoroughly evil and violent that God actually regretted He had created human beings. The story is recorded in the Book of Genesis.

> Then the Lord saw that the wickedness of man was great in the earth, and that every intent of the thoughts of his heart was only evil continually. And the Lord was sorry that He had made man on the earth, and He was grieved in His heart. So the Lord said, "I will destroy man whom I have created from the face of the earth, both man and beast, creeping thing and birds of the air, for I am sorry that I have made them." . . . The earth also was corrupt before God, and the earth was filled with violence. So God looked upon the earth, and indeed it was corrupt; for all flesh had corrupted their way on the earth (Genesis 6:5-7, 11-12).

In that violent and wicked world, Noah was the only man who found grace in the eyes of the Lord,[10] and God spared his family from the destruction of the Flood. But even though all of those who had lived violently and corruptly were gone and life began again, evil still remained on the earth. Since the Tower of Babel, the entire history of the world has been characterized by violence, immorality . . . in short, by the complete spectrum of evil.

This Is Not What God Wants

The world as it exists today is not what God intended. It is not what He wants. And it is not how it always will be. But until the time when evil is eradicated, what is to be the attitude of those who believe in God?

Jesus said, "These things I have spoken to you, that in Me you may have peace. In the world you will have tribulation; but be of good cheer, I have overcome the world" (John 16:33). Paul wrote, "For our light affliction, which is but for a moment, is working for us a far more exceeding and eternal weight of glory" (II Corinthians 4:17). In Peter's words, we should "greatly rejoice, though now for a little while, if need be, [we] have been grieved by various trials, that the genuineness of [our] faith, being much more precious than gold that perishes, though it is tested by fire, may be found to praise, honor, and glory at the revelation of Jesus Christ" (I Peter 1:6-7). Further, Peter wrote that "when [we] do good and suffer, if [we] take it patiently, this is commendable before God. For to this [we] were called, because Christ also suffered for us, leaving us an example, that we should follow His steps" (I Peter 2:20-21). As our example, Christ did not revile those who reviled Him. When He suffered, He did not threaten those who afflicted Him. Rather, He committed everything to God, the righteous judge.[11] In his profound treatment of the topic of suffering, Peter described it as something believers can expect.

Beloved, do not think it strange concerning the fiery trial which is to try you, as though some strange thing happened to you; but rejoice to the extent that you partake of Christ's sufferings, that when His glory is revealed, you may also be glad with exceeding joy. If you are reproached for the name of Christ, blessed are you, for the Spirit of glory and of God rests upon you. On their part He is blasphemed, but on your part He is glorified. But let none of you suffer as a murderer, a thief, an evildoer, or as a busybody in other people's matters. Yet if anyone suffers as a Christian, let him not be ashamed, but let him glorify God in this matter. . . . Therefore let those who suffer according to the will of God commit their souls to Him in doing good, as to a faithful Creator (I Peter 4:12-16, 19).

Many biblical scholars believe the Book of James is the earliest New Testament book to be written. If so, it seems quite significant that the first New Testament book addresses the issue of trials immediately after its opening salutation. James wrote, "My brethren, count it all joy when you fall into various trials, knowing that the testing of your faith produces patience. But let patience have its perfect work, that you may be perfect and complete, lacking nothing" (James 1:2-4).

In the following chapters, we will explore what the Bible says about the universal nature of suffering, what our response to suffering should be, and how God can use even the most painful circumstances to bring about things of lasting value in our lives.

23

2
Trusting God in Our Suffering

Pain and suffering are facts of life. David wrote, "Many are the afflictions of the righteous, but the Lord delivers him out of them all" (Psalm 34:19).[12] We can attest to the many afflictions experienced by those who believe, but we may wonder about the statement, "The Lord delivers him out of them all."

According to Jewish tradition, Psalm 34 reflects David's experiences when he pretended madness before "Abimelech."[13] This episode occurred in David's flight from Saul's wrath. Armed with Goliath's sword, which he had obtained from a priest, David fled to Achish, the king of Gath. But the servants of Achish recognized David, and when they informed the king of his identity, David "was very much afraid of Achish" (I Samuel 21:12). Seeing that it had been a mistake to seek refuge in Gath, David tried to deflect any intent Achish might have to harm him and "changed his behavior before them, pretended madness in their hands, scratched on the doors of the gate, and let his saliva fall down on his beard" (I Samuel 21:13). Achish smirked and said to his servants, "Look, you see the man is insane. Why have you brought him to me? Have I need of madmen, that you have brought this fellow to play the madman in my presence? Shall this fellow come into my house?" (I Samuel 21:14-15).

In this case, the Lord delivered David from possible harm by giving David the idea to feign madness. But David's psalm makes no promise as to how or when God will deliver the righteous. It is one thing to know God delivers the righteous from affliction; it would be another thing to know exactly how or when He would do this. Biblical history indicates that some that were righteous were never delivered on this earth; their deliverance from pain and suffering came only through death, and their ultimate deliverance awaits the resurrection.

Hebrews 11 is known by many as "Faith's Hall of Fame." Most of the chapter tells the story of people of faith who, as a result of their faith in God, experienced a wide variety of miracles, including deliverance from all kinds of danger. For example, some of them, through faith, "stopped the mouths of lions," as did Daniel, "quenched the violence of fire," as did Shadrach, Meshach, and Abed-Nego, "out of weakness were made strong, became valiant in battle, turned to flight the armies of the aliens" and "[w]omen received their dead raised to life again" (Hebrews 11:33b-35a). But this is not the end of the story. Others, who were equally people of faith, "were tortured, not accepting deliverance, that they might obtain a better resurrection. Still others had trial of mockings and scourgings, yes, and of chains and imprisonment. They were stoned, they were sawn in two," as was Isaiah, according to Jewish tradition, "were tempted, were slain with the sword. They wandered about in sheepskins and goatskins, being destitute, afflicted, tormented" (Hebrews 11:35-37).

We might at first think the stories of miraculous victories recorded in most of Hebrews 11 are proof of the genuineness of the faith of these people, while the stories of suffering, defeat, and death evidence the lack of faith of the rest. But we would be wrong. One conclusion to draw from Hebrews 11 is that it is impossible to determine whether somebody is a person of faith by the circumstances of that person's life. Indeed, the chapter concludes after describing these sufferers with these words: ". . . of whom the world was not worthy. They wandered in deserts and mountains, in dens and caves of the earth. And all these, having obtained a good testimony through faith, did not receive the promise" (Hebrews 11:38-39).

These words may sound quite strange to us. We are used to connecting faith with receiving promises. In fact, some of the people of faith mentioned in Hebrews 11 did receive what God promised them.[14] But others did not. Oh, they will someday. God keeps His promises. But sometimes, in view of the greater purposes and plans of the sovereign God, people of faith must live in the land of pending promises.

I remember standing by the bed of a dear friend, a man of faith. He was suffering with diabetes, and the doctors were considering the possibility of amputation. As we discussed this bleak prognosis and prepared to pray, my friend uttered one of the most profound statements I have ever heard on the subject of faith. He said, "I guess faith is different things to different people. But to me, faith is knowing that God will do what is right for me." It almost seemed I was hearing the voice of God from that hospital bed.

Putting It in Perspective

The apostle Paul was a man of great faith, but he was no stranger to pain and suffering. Listen to the following excerpt from his words on this subject.

But in all things we commend ourselves as ministers of God: in much patience, in tribulations, in needs, in distresses, in

27

stripes, in imprisonments, in tumults, in labors, in sleeplessness, in fastings . . . by honor and dishonor, by evil report
and good report . . . as dying . . . as chastened . . . as sorrow-
ful . . . as poor . . . as having nothing.

. . . in labors more abundant, in stripes above measure, in
prisons more frequently, in deaths often. From the Jews
five times I received forty stripes minus one. Three times I
was beaten with rods; once I was stoned; three times I was
shipwrecked; a night and a day I have been in the deep; in
journeys often, in perils of waters, in perils of robbers, in
perils of my own countrymen, in perils of the Gentiles, in
perils in the city, in perils in the wilderness, in perils in the
sea, in perils among false brethren; in weariness and toil, in
sleeplessness often, in hunger and thirst, in fastings often,
in cold and nakedness (II Corinthians 6:4-10; 11:23b-27).

Words like these make us uncomfortable. We would rather
read bright, cheerful, and encouraging words.

Did you ever notice that words like these are never found
in promise boxes? Remember the promise boxes? They were
usually made of ceramic and shaped to resemble a loaf of
bread. A slot in the top was just the right size to insert little
cards imprinted with various verses of Scripture. Those scriptural quotes were selected without any regard for the contexts
in which the verses were found, and they never included any
hint of suffering and pain. When you went to the promise box,
you could always count on getting good news. But the Bible
was not written in the form of a promise box. It did not come
to us as a series of little cards, each of which offered a cheerful
pick-me-up for the day. Although the Bible has a great deal of
good news, not least of which is the gospel message itself, it
deals with life as it is. The Bible deals with reality, not with

a pain-free, peaceful, healthy and wealthy society that exists nowhere on planet earth.

Paul understood what it means to be a person of faith in a suffering world. In addition to what we have already read from his pen, Paul wrote the following words.

We are hard pressed on every side, yet not crushed; we are perplexed, but not in despair; persecuted, but not forsaken; struck down, but not destroyed—always carrying about in the body the dying of the Lord Jesus, that the life of Jesus also may be manifested in our body. For we who live are always delivered to death for Jesus' sake, that the life of Jesus also may be manifested in our mortal flesh. . . . Therefore we do not lose heart. Even though our outward man is perishing, yet the inward man is being renewed day by day. For our light affliction, which is but for a moment, is working for us a far more exceeding and eternal weight of glory, while we do not look at the things which are seen, but at the things which are not seen. For the things which are seen are temporary, but the things which are not seen are eternal (II Corinthians 4:8-11, 16-18).

We may be tempted to lose heart when we are hard pressed, perplexed, persecuted, and struck down. "Losing heart" is the sensation of being crushed, in despair, forsaken, and destroyed. But we can keep our perspective in the midst of suffering if we remember that our affliction—compared to the "weight" of the glory to come—is "light." Compared to the "eternal" nature of the glory to come, our affliction is "but for a moment."

Evidently our affliction in some way identifies us with Jesus; we carry about in our body "the dying of the Lord Jesus." We are "delivered to death for Jesus' sake." This is to

29

result in "the life of Jesus" being "manifested in our body." As the "outward man is perishing," "the inward man is being renewed day by day." This temporary, light affliction is "working for us." It will produce for us something of eternal value. But in order for us to grasp this, we must "look at the things which are not seen" rather than "the things which are seen." As long as we stay focused on our pain and suffering, we will miss the potential comfort to be gained by looking heavenward.

A Biblical View of Pain and Suffering

To begin to understand pain and suffering from a biblical point of view, we must first be aware of God's attributes. Then we must understand what it means to be human. The pain and suffering we experience are the consequences of being broken people in a broken world. God's interaction with us in our pain and suffering is determined by the fact that He is the perfect, holy Creator whose interaction with His creation reflects His wholeness and our brokenness.

The attributes of God particularly relevant to a biblical understanding of pain and suffering include His omnipotence, or the fact that He is all powerful; His omnipresence, which means there is no place where God is not; His omniscience, meaning that God is all knowing; His eternality, which tells us that God has no beginning and no ending; His immutability, or the fact that He does not change. We must also consider His sovereignty, love, justice, truth, freedom, and holiness.

Omnipotence

In 1779, the Scottish philosopher David Hume wrote, "Is God willing to prevent evil, but not able? then he is impotent. Is he able, but not willing? then he is malevolent. Is he both able and willing? whence then is evil?"[15] As people view the suffering in our world, or as they personally endure suffering, they may ask, "If there is a good God, and if He has all power, how could He let this happen?" Since suffering abounds, some conclude either that there is no God, or that if He exists He must not be a good God, or that if He is a good God, He must not be able to stop the suffering. These questions reflect a lack of understanding of the nature of God and the nature of human beings.

The Bible declares God has all power: "Alleluia! For the Lord God Omnipotent reigns!" (Revelation 19:6b). Since God is all powerful, He can do whatever He wants insofar as it is consistent with His character and in harmony with His purposes. Even though He is omnipotent, there are some things God cannot do. For example, He cannot be tempted by evil. James wrote, "Let no one say when he is tempted, 'I am tempted by God'; for God cannot be tempted by evil, nor does He Himself tempt anyone" (James 1:13). God cannot lie. In his letter to Titus, Paul wrote of the hope of eternal life "which God, who cannot lie, promised before time began" (Titus 1:2). These things are inconsistent with His character. He cannot save people on any basis other than the blood of Jesus. Paul wrote, "In Him we have redemption through his blood, the forgiveness of sins, according to the riches of His grace" (Ephesians 1:7). To save anyone on any other basis would not be in harmony with God's purpose.[16]31

Neither can God perform a logical contradiction. In an attempt to undermine the omnipotence of God, some have asked, "Can God make a rock so heavy He cannot lift it?" This is like asking, "Can God make a square circle?"

Since the omnipotence of God works within the framework of His character and purposes, God's interaction with humans in their pain and suffering is influenced by the image of God in humans. God has the ability to do whatever He wants as long as it is consistent with His image in mankind. Even though He is all-powerful, God cannot compromise the genuineness of His image in humans.

The omnipotence of God means that human pain and suffering cannot be explained by any claim that God is weak and incapable of doing good. Human suffering does not indicate divine weakness.

Omniscience

Not only is God all powerful, He is also all knowing. David affirmed that the Lord knows every detail of our lives.

> O Lord, You have searched me and known me. You know my sitting down and my rising up; You understand my thought afar off. You comprehend my path and my lying down, and are acquainted with all my ways. For there is not a word on my tongue, but behold, O Lord, You know it altogether. You have hedged me behind and before, and laid Your hand upon me. Such knowledge is too wonderful for me; it is high, I cannot attain it (Psalm 139:1-6).

This indeed is wonderful knowledge, beyond human comprehension. Since we are not omniscient, we cannot fathom how God can know everything there is to know. Nothing is outside the realm of His knowledge. According to John, God "knows all things" (I John 3:20). His eyes "are in every place, keeping watch on the evil and the good" (Proverbs 15:3). God's knowledge is so complete, He knows when a sparrow falls and even has numbered the hairs of our head. (See Matthew 10:29-30.)

Since God knows all there is to know, He is fully aware of our suffering. The fact of our suffering does not indicate any limitation in God's knowledge. It is inappropriate to think that if God only knew, He would do something about it. He does know. Our perception of whether He is doing anything about it may not be accurate, but the suffering is not occurring due to unawareness on God's part.

Eternality

The names of God describe some aspect of His essence or subsistence. Essence has to do with God's essential nature; subsistence has to do with how He exists, especially in relationship to Himself and to His creation.

One of His names is El Olam, which means "Everlasting God,"[17] He is "the King eternal" (I Timothy 1:17). He "inhabits eternity" (Isaiah 57:15). God exists above and beyond His creation "from everlasting to everlasting" (Psalm 90:2). His memorial name "I AM" may imply His eternality.[18]33

Since God has no point of origin or termination, and since He transcends time, He is at once fully aware of the entire scope of human history. He is also fully aware of the entire scope of eternity, although we cannot comprehend this.

From eternity, God has known everything He would do. At the first church council in about AD 50, James said, "Known to God from eternity are all His works" (Acts 15:18). Not only does God know everything that has happened, is happening, and will happen, He also knows what would have happened if things had been different than they are! For example, Jesus rebuked some of the cities where He had done most of His mighty works.

Woe to you, Chorazin! Woe to you, Bethsaida! For if the mighty works which were done in you had been done in Tyre and Sidon, they would have repented long ago in sackcloth and ashes. But I say to you, it will be more toler-able for Tyre and Sidon in the day of judgment than for you. And you, Capernaum, who are exalted to heaven, will be brought down to Hades; for if the mighty works which were done in you had been done in Sodom, it would have remained until this day. But I say to you that it shall be more tolerable for the land of Sodom in the day of judgment than for you (Matthew 11:21-24).

Since God is eternal, He not only knows all the details of an episode of suffering as it develops, but He also is fully aware of all the events that may have led up to an episode of suffering. He is aware of how the episode may end, and He knows any effects it will have on the sufferer and those around the sufferer.

God's eternality means it's inappropriate to think if only God had known where circumstances were leading, He could have or would have done something to stop them before they culminated in an episode of suffering. The fact of suffering does not mean God is bound by time and the suffering sur-prised Him as much as it surprised us.

Recently, some theologians suggested that classical doc-trines about God need to be reexamined. These include God's immutability and His foreknowledge. These scholars, who describe their idea as "the openness of God," deal in part with the problem of evil by saying God doesn't know certain things about the future. They say, for example, God's "omniscience need not mean exhaustive foreknowledge of all future events. If that were its meaning, the future would be fixed and determined, much as is the past. . . . It also would imply that human freedom is an illusion, that we make no difference and are not respon-sible."[19] Thus, God is just as surprised by accidents and violent

34

acts as we are. If He had known about them in advance, He could have done something to prevent them, but He didn't know.

This idea may bring a measure of comfort to some people who question how God could have allowed some horrible tragedy, but it does so at the cost of diminishing and weakening their perception of God. The prophet Isaiah recorded these words of God: "Remember the former things of old, for I am God, and there is no other; I am God, and there is none like Me, declaring the end from the beginning, and from ancient times things that are not yet done, saying, 'My counsel shall stand, and I will do all My pleasure'" (Isaiah 46:9-10). The New Testament speaks specifically of God's foreknowledge in four different texts.[20] We are familiar with the Greek word prognosis in these texts. Literally, the word means "to know beforehand" or "to know in advance."

Whatever we are going to say about the problem of suffering, it cannot violate what Scripture tells us about the kind of God revealed in the Bible. It can't take away His omnipotence; God possesses all power. It can't minimize His omniscience; God knows all there is to know. It can't compromise his eternality; there was never a time when God was not, and there will never be a time when He will not be.

In the following chapters, we will continue to examine the significance of God's attributes in developing a biblical view of suffering. We will also look at human nature, including the impact of the Fall, to see how this influences our experiences of pain and suffering.

In the meantime, be assured that regardless of the pain and suffering you may be experiencing at this moment, God cares for you deeply and loves you more than you can know. This wonderful and comforting truth is preserved in the following immortal words of the apostle Paul.

For I am persuaded that neither death nor life, nor angels nor principalities nor powers, nor things present nor things to come, nor height nor depth, nor any other created thing, shall be able to separate us from the love of God which is in Christ Jesus our Lord (Romans 8:38-39).

3

God's Nature and Human Nature

A s believers, our questions about human suffering inevitably involve God. Why does He allow suffering? Is He able but unwilling to alleviate suffering? Is He willing, but unable? What does our suffering tell us about God?

Thinking carefully about our suffering presents another line of questions. What does our suffering tell us about human beings? How much suffering is a consequence of broken relationships between human beings, whether personal relationships, subcultures, or nations? How much suffering is due to self-abuse, carelessness, neglect, or other causes that could have been avoided? How much suffering is beyond our control?

We may think that in an ideal world, suffering would be eliminated altogether. But we must live with reality: we are broken people living in a broken world.

A Biblical View of Suffering

To resolve our questions about God's involvement or seeming lack of it in our suffering, we must consider how God's attributes influence His interaction with us.[21] We've already noted His omnipotence doesn't mean He can do anything. It means He can do anything He wishes, insofar as it's

37

consistent with His character and in harmony with His purposes. He cannot perform a logical contradiction. As it relates to His interaction with humans, He can do whatever He wants insofar as it corresponds with His image in human beings. He can't act in such a way as to compromise the genuineness of His image in humans.

We've also considered the implications of God's omniscience. Scripture affirms that God knows everything there is to know. Thus, He is fully aware of our suffering and pain. It is wrong to think, If only God knew, He would do something about it. He does know. Perhaps we are wrong to think He's doing nothing about our situation.

In addition, we've thought about God's eternality. He inhabits eternity and has no point of origin or termination. Since He transcends time, God is fully aware of the past, present, and future. But that isn't all. He also knows what would have happened if things had been different than they are.

Imagine trying to play a game of chess with God. He not only knows your next move, He also knows every conceivable move you could make. In addition, He knows every possible response He could make to each move you could make. This is true for each move in the entire game until it ends in checkmate or a draw. I haven't found an authoritative statement about how many possible moves are in a game of chess. Experts differ in their estimates. According to one estimate, each side has 318,979,564,000 possibilities in the first four moves. One expert says the number of possible moves per game is ten to the tenth power to the fiftieth power. Ten to the tenth power is 10 billion. I have no idea what 10 billion to the fiftieth power is. But I do know it's impossible to beat God at a game of chess if He intends to win the game.

Concerning God's omniscience, some students of the Bible think if God knows everything that will happen in the future, it means He has predestined everything and nothing can be changed. Some people respond to this idea by giving up. They say, "If God already knows whether I will be saved or lost, what's the use of trying?" Others respond by appealing to God's sovereignty. Let's consider His sovereignty for a moment.

Sovereignty

The Bible teaches that God is in control of all He has made. Nothing happens that has not been decreed or permitted by Him. God has a purpose, and He "works all things according to the counsel of His will" (Ephesians 1:11). Not only does His sovereignty extend to the grand sweep of the rise and fall of nations, it also includes even the most personal realms of existence and experience.[22] God said to Moses, "Who has made man's mouth? Or who makes the mute, the deaf, the seeing, or the blind? Have not I, the Lord?" (Exodus 4:11). When Jesus passed a man who had been born blind, His disciples asked, "Rabbi, who sinned, this man or his parents, that he was born blind?" (John 9:1). For years I puzzled over this question. How could Jesus' disciples think this man was born blind because of his own sin? Then I discovered that some first-century Pharisees taught it was possible to sin while still in the womb. But Jesus' answer proved this question was completely wrong. He said, "Neither this man nor his parents sinned, but that the works of God should be revealed in him" (John 9:3).

Although it's widely recognized that God is sovereign, theologians differ as to how the sovereignty of God works. Some believe He has decreed from eternity everything that will ever happen, to the smallest detail. In this view, God determined every thought, word, and action of every human being before He made anything. In the realm of "nature," God determined from eternity precisely how tall each blade of grass would grow, how many houses each tornado would destroy and which ones, and so forth. According to this view, for humans to have free choice means that from eternity, God decreed the specific events and influences in each person's life so that the person will "freely" choose what God decreed. Others suppose God decreed certain events in broad strokes so as to allow for complete freedom of human choice while still accomplishing His purposes. This is the way I understand God's sovereignty.

I remember sitting in a seminary class one day as we discussed God's foreknowledge. The professor thought God predestined every happening, including every word we speak and whether or not we will be saved. To illustrate his point, he joked, "If you believe in predestination, what do you say after you fall down the stairs? You say, 'Thank God that's over!'" Just as the professor finished the joke, he shifted his body and nearly fell off the stool where he sat. I couldn't resist saying, "Thank God that's over!"

Scripture definitely teaches that God knows the future. But I could never understand why some people think if God knows the future, that means He has predestined everything that will happen. In my mind, it's one thing to know what will happen; it's quite another to predetermine every decision that will ever be made and each event in the entire scope of human history. To those who embrace the idea of divine predestination of every detail, this makes God an awesome, powerful, sovereign God. I agree that a God who could micromanage every detail of the universe, including every thought I would ever think, every word I would ever say, and the height of every blade of grass would be an awesome God. But it's quite clear God has given human beings complete freedom of choice because they are made in the image of God. This was demonstrated in the

40

Garden of Eden when God created the tree of the knowledge
of good and evil and warned Adam against eating its fruit,
but permitted him to do so. In my view it's even more awesome when God grants complete freedom of choice to human
beings and can still bring to pass His purposes regardless of
the choices they make.

It was clearly not the will of God for Adam and Eve to eat
of the forbidden tree. Therefore, it's unfathomable that God
would command Adam not to eat of the tree although He had
predestined him to do so. No matter how we try to explain this,
Adam would not have had a truly free choice, and God would,
at least to some degree, be the author of sin. But the point is,
even though it was not the will of God for Adam to eat the
forbidden fruit, God is still able to bring to pass His purposes
in the world in spite of Adam's disobedience.

No human analogy can adequately explain anything about
God, much less His omniscience, eternality, and foreknowledge and how these attributes work in conjunction with the
human freedom of choice. I've often used a little story from my
family to try to illustrate at least something of how this works.

Many years ago, when our children were small, my wife,
Judy, and I purposed to take one day a week with our two
children to relax and enjoy one another. At that time, I was the
pastor of a church. We also operated a Christian school and had
many other ministry responsibilities. One Monday it occurred
to us that we hadn't taken any time off with our children for
quite a while, so Judy and I agreed to take our children to Six
Flags the following Thursday. We also agreed we would not
tell the children in advance; we would surprise them. So on
Thursday morning, I went into our son's bedroom and woke
him up with these words: "Mark, today is your day. We'll do
anything you want. What would you like to do?" In a flash,
Mark, who was about eight or nine years old, said, "Let's go

to Six Flags!" I answered, "Fine! That's just what we'll do!" Judy and I had already planned to spend the day at Six Flags, but I knew my son well enough to know if I let him decide, he would choose Six Flags as well. Now, theoretically, Mark could have chosen anything. He could have said, "Let's go to the zoo." If he had done so, I would have had to try to convince him he really wanted to go to Six Flags, or I would have had to take him to the zoo, since I had given my word. This little story is just an analogy, and an imperfect one. But God knows us better than I know my son. God gives us complete freedom of choice, but He knows what choices we'll make. This doesn't mean He predestines us to make those choices; it just means He knows us very well.

What does all this mean for those who are suffering? The omniscience of God means He knows the pain we're going through. The sovereignty of God means He has either ordained the suffering for some specific reason—as in the case of Job and other sufferers whose stories are recorded in Scripture—or He has allowed it to occur within the broad parameters of His purpose either in the context of our fallenness or as a consequence of our having been created in the image of God with the freedom of choice.

Now, we also need to talk about God's immutability. How does this divine attribute connect with our experiences of pain and suffering?

Immutability

To say God is immutable is to say He doesn't change. He is not "in process." The Lord Himself declared, "For I am the Lord, I do not change" (Malachi 3:6). With the Father, there is "no variation or shadow of turning" (James 1:17). Jesus Christ is the same yesterday, today, and forever (Hebrews 13:8). Not only is God immutable; so is His counsel. "Thus

42

God, determining to show more abundantly to the heirs of promise the immutability of His counsel, confirmed it by an oath" (Hebrews 6:17).

Since God does not change, we can state with certainty that, in His dealings with His creation, He is impartial, consistent, and blameless. We may not know the full extent of His involvement with any events leading up to an episode of suffering (i.e., we can know only what He chooses to reveal [Deuteronomy 29:29]), and we can't predict any interaction He may have with those who suffer, but our uncertainty is not due to any change in God. Our uncertainties are due only to the limitations of human knowledge.

It's a comfort to know God is not arbitrary or capricious. He isn't governed by moods or prejudice. As Peter discovered, "God shows no partiality" (Acts 10:34). Any involvement He may or may not have with us in our suffering is due to His consistency. It may seem to us that life is not fair, but to the extent He can be engaged with us in view of His nature and His respect for His image in us, God is blameless. In the midst of his suffering, David prayed, "That You may be found just when You speak, and blameless when You judge" (Psalm 51:4b).

The divine attributes we've examined so far are commonly called His incommunicable attributes. This means they belong to God alone; they cannot be communicated to human beings. For example, humans will never be omnipotent, omniscient, or sovereign. But God has other attributes that are communicable to human beings. These also must be considered in our effort to gain a biblical understanding of the problem of suffering and pain. The first of them is love.

Love

Twice, John wrote, "God is love" (I John 4:8, 16). The word translated "love" is agapē, which might be practically defined as "selfless concern for the well-being of another." The classic passage that explains agapē is I Corinthians 13. When we look at this biblical definition of love, we realize it's far more than the sentimental romanticism so often portrayed in Hollywood productions.

> Love suffers long and is kind; love does not envy; love does not parade itself, is not puffed up; does not behave rudely, does not seek its own, is not provoked, thinks no evil; does not rejoice in iniquity, but rejoices in the truth; bears all things, believes all things, hopes all things, endures all things. Love never fails (I Corinthians 13:4-8a).

The ultimate demonstration of God's love is His gift of His Son to provide for our salvation. This is described in perhaps the best-known verse in the Bible: "For God so loved the world that He gave His only begotten Son, that whoever believes in Him should not perish but have everlasting life" (John 3:16). John said even more about this in his first letter: "In this the love of God was manifested toward us, that God has sent His only begotten Son into the world, that we might live through Him. In this is love, not that we loved God, but that He loved us and sent His Son to be the propitiation for our sins. Beloved, if God so loved us, we also ought to love one another" (I John 4:9-11). Since love is the most precious gift He could give, it assures that God will freely give us all other things that contribute to our well-being. Paul put it this way: "He who did not spare His own Son, but delivered Him up for us all, how shall He not with Him also freely give us all things?" (Romans 8:32). When I say God will freely give us all things that contribute to our well-being, I'm referring to the Hebrew idea of shalom ("peace"), which has to do with wholeness in every aspect of our existence, whether spiritually, socially, emotionally, mentally, or physically. In other words, God's gift of His Son assures us He will go to any extent possible to bring us to a place of wholeness, as defined by Him. Our idea of "well-being" and His idea of "well-being" may be quite different.

Since God is love, no matter what He ordains or permits to come into our lives, His intent is to demonstrate His love for us and to contribute ultimately to our well-being. It may be virtually impossible for us to recognize this as we endure a specific episode of suffering, and God accepts that, He doesn't expect us to enjoy suffering. Jesus Himself did not enjoy suffering. The Book of Hebrews tells us that Jesus, "in the days of His flesh, when He had offered up prayers and supplications, with vehement cries and tears to Him who was able to save Him from death, and was heard because of His godly fear, though He was a Son, yet He learned obedience by the things which He suffered" (Hebrews 5:7-8).[23]

Both the imprecatory and lament Psalms evidence the human inability to readily recognize the hand of God in our suffering. Since these psalms are divinely inspired, they also prove that God accepts our questions—even our questions of Him—and expressions of negative emotions in the midst of our pain.[24] Perhaps no better example of this can be seen than in the Book of Lamentations.

A lamentation is a complaint, which means we have in our Bible a book of inspired complaints. Some people have the idea it's wrong for Christians ever to complain. Some even urge us to confess things to be other than they are in our lives, thinking that somehow words create reality. They support this idea by taking verses out of their context or by attributing God's creative power to human beings. For example, some claim, by appealing to Romans 4:17, we can call nonexistent things into existence. But a careful examination of the verse and its context shows only God can do this. God called Abraham the father of many nations before Abraham had even one descendant because God can give life to the dead and call those things which do not exist as though they did.

If the Holy Spirit inspired Jeremiah to write an entire book of complaints, it's obviously acceptable with God for us to be honest about our situation when we experience pain and suffering. The Book of Lamentations is quite bleak. It is, as someone said, the funeral of a city. Jeremiah, who remained in Jerusalem after Babylon invaded and destroyed the city, is rightly called the weeping prophet. Not only were the city and the Temple completely demolished, but civilization itself lost its veneer of decency. And Jeremiah made it clear all of this happened because of God's judgment on Jerusalem for its sins. But in the middle of this precisely structured book—notice how each chapter has twenty-two verses except the middle chapter, which has sixty-six—in the midst of all the smoke, blood, death, starvation, and violence, we read these words: "For He does not afflict willingly, nor grieve the children of men" (Lamentations 3:33). It's true that Jerusalem's destruction was due to sin, but even then, the affliction was not God's will. God would much rather bless than afflict.

When I looked at the Hebrew text of Lamentations 3:33, I discovered an amazing thing. The literal translation of the verse would be, "For God does not afflict from His heart." When God afflicts, even for sin, it doesn't show us God's heart. God's heart is shown to us in His love. Although Scripture talks about the wrath of God, it never tells us God is wrath. It does tell us God is love. Even God's judgment is tempered by His love.

46

We shouldn't be surprised when we find it difficult to see the hand of God in our experiences of intense pressure, distress, or persecution for our faith. If we lack adequate food or clothing, it may be hard to think any good could be found in such a circumstance. Where's the hand of God in life-threatening danger? Can we possibly see God's love in the death of someone dear to us?

Experiences like these may lead us to think there are—after all—limits to God's sovereignty, or His concern for us, or His ability to help us. Instead, we should expect experiences of suffering, and we must not interpret them to mean God no longer loves us![25]

The fact that God is love means, regardless of the nature of our suffering, God is faithful and loyal in His love for us. However painful our situation may be, we must not take it to mean God is unconcerned. He intends that every experience will ultimately accomplish His good purposes for us. We could view these experiences as a consequence of His gift of the freedom of choice.[26]

In the following chapters, we will further examine the relationship between the communicable or moral attributes of God and His involvement with us in our suffering.

4

Attributes Common to God and People

In previous chapters, we've looked at how some of the incommunicable attributes of God influence His interaction with us in our suffering. Certain of God's attributes are called "incommunicable" because they are unique to God; humans do not experience them in any way.

We noted that His omnipotence means He can do whatever He wants insofar as it corresponds with His character, harmonizes with His purposes, and reflects His image in humans. He cannot perform logical contradictions. Our suffering cannot be explained by any claim that God is weak and incapable of doing good. Since God is omniscient, He knows every detail of our lives, thus He's fully aware of our suffering. Our suffering cannot be explained by saying God would do something about it if only He knew; He does know. The eternality of God means He transcends time; He is at once fully aware of the entire scope of human history. This means He's fully aware of all of the events that may have led up to an episode of suffering, and He knows how that episode may terminate and its long-term effects on all involved. It's wrong to think, If only God knew this would end in suffering, He would have done something about it. As it relates to our suffering, the immutability of God

49

means He is not arbitrary or capricious. We need not fear He caused our suffering because of His prejudice or moods. He's perfectly consistent. Since God is sovereign, He is in control of all creation. This means that, for His own reasons, He has either ordained or permitted each specific episode of suffering.

In chapter 3, we began looking at the relationship between our suffering and God's communicable attributes, or those attributes humans can experience to some degree. First, we examined love. We saw that God is love, so anything He permits to come into our lives demonstrates His love for us and contributes ultimately to our well-being. We may not recognize this at first, and that's OK with God. We noted that an inspired book in the Bible bears the title "Book of Complaints." Precisely in the center of that book, better known as the Book of Lamentations, is the good news that God does not afflict from His heart.

Now we'll continue looking at the relationship between God's communicable attributes and our suffering. First, let's consider the attribute of justice.

Justice

As Abraham interacted with God concerning the impending destruction of Sodom and Gomorrah, he said, "Suppose there were fifty righteous within the city; would You also destroy the place and not spare it for the fifty righteous that were in it? Far be it from You to do such a thing as this, to slay the righteous with the wicked, so that the righteous should be as the wicked; far be it from You! Shall not the Judge of all the earth do right?" (Genesis 18:24-25). Abraham instinctively understood the justice of God; God will do what is right. The Lord responded, "If I find in Sodom fifty righteous within the city, then I will spare all the place for their sakes" (Genesis 18:26).

But Abraham wasn't finished. He continued, "Indeed now, I who am but dust and ashes have taken it upon myself to speak to the Lord: Suppose there were five less than the fifty righteous; would You destroy all of the city for lack of five?" God answered, "If I find there are forty-five, I will not destroy it" (Genesis 18:27-28). But Abraham had more to ask: "Suppose there should be forty found there?" God answered, "I will not do it for the sake of forty" (Genesis 18:29). Perhaps sensing he was close to pressing the question too much, Abraham said, "Let not the Lord be angry, and I will speak: Suppose thirty should be found there?" "I will not do it if I find thirty there," said God (Genesis 18:30). It's quite easy to see where this story is headed. Abraham ventured another question: "Indeed now, I have taken it upon myself to speak to the Lord: Suppose twenty should be found there?" Again, God's answer was positive: "I will not destroy it for the sake of twenty" (Genesis 18:31). One last time, Abraham tested the boundaries. He said, "Let not the Lord be angry, and I will speak but once more: Suppose ten should be found there?" God responded, "I will not destroy it for the sake of ten" (Genesis 18:32-33).

Everyone who knows the story of Sodom and Gomorrah knows not even ten righteous people could be found there. I wonder what God would have said if Abraham had asked about five, or two, or even one. Regardless of that, Abraham understood this divine characteristic: God is just. He will do the right thing.

Paul wrote that God "has appointed a day on which He will judge the world in righteousness" (Acts 17:31). This means God will judge rightly.

The justice of God has to do with His moral equity. Just as God's immutability assures us He is not capricious or prejudiced, so does His justice. He is no respecter of persons.[27]

51

His justice means He bases His treatment of each person on what's right in that particular circumstance and considering all factors—including those known to us and those known only to Him. As Paul put it, "There is no partiality with God. For as many as have sinned without law will also perish without law, and as many as have sinned in the law will be judged by the law" (Romans 2:11-12). In other words, each person is responsible for what he knows. God doesn't hold people responsible for something they never knew. This doesn't mean people will be saved because they didn't know what they should do, but it does means God will take into account each person's uniqueness rather than dealing with each person in precisely the same way. It may at first seem if God isn't partial He would treat everyone the same. But the reverse is true. If God treated everyone in exactly the same way, regardless of their circumstances, that would be partiality, because some have greater opportunities than others.

Jesus addressed this issue: "That servant who knew his master's will, and did not prepare himself or do according to his will, shall be beaten with many stripes. But he who did not know, yet committed things deserving of stripes, shall be beaten with few. For everyone to whom much is given, from him much will be required" (Luke 12:47-48). Also, Jesus said it would be more tolerable in the Day of Judgment for Sodom, Tyre, and Sidon than for Capernaum, Chorazin, and Bethsaida. The reason is the people of Sodom, Tyre, and Sidon would have repented if they had the opportunities of the people of Capernaum, Chorazin, and Bethsaida.[28]

Even eternal rewards will take into account how believers exercised their freedom of choice. Paul discussed how we build our Christian life on the foundation of Jesus Christ in I Corinthians 3.

Now if anyone builds on this foundation with gold, silver, precious stones, wood, hay, straw, each one's work will become clear; for the Day will declare it, because it will be revealed by fire; and the fire will test each one's work, of what sort it is. If anyone's work which he has built on it endures, he will receive a reward. If anyone's work is burned, he will suffer loss; but he himself will be saved, yet so as through fire (I Corinthians 3:12-15).

The point is that even though God shows no partiality, He won't reward everyone in precisely the same way on the Day of Judgment. He will take into account the quality of their work. The bad news is, some people will suffer loss. The good news is, they will nevertheless be saved. Although they are saved by grace through faith and not of works, since salvation is a gift (Ephesians 2:8), their rewards will be based on whether their work was in the category of gold, silver, and precious stones, or wood, hay, and straw. God shows no partiality; His interaction with each person reflects that person's uniqueness, whether it has to do with the level of revelation that person receives or with the quality of his or her work as they live out the Christian life.

As it relates to our suffering, God's justice assures us He is not abusing, manipulating, or in any way treating us wrongly. It may seem to us at the time that injustice has prevailed, but that's a matter of perception only. From His all-wise, eternal perspective, God makes certain that right prevails.

Now let's consider another communicable attribute of God: truth.

Truth

Jesus said, "I am the way, the truth, and the life" (John 14:6). For God to be truth means more than that He cannot lie. It means everything He ordains or permits is consistent with His character. God will never deceive those who love Him. Although God may deceive His enemies,[29] even this harmonizes with His character. His enemies have set themselves against Him; they are at war with Him, and the nature of warfare is to mislead the enemy.

Even as believers, we may sometimes feel God has deceived us. Jeremiah said, "Ah, Lord God! Surely You have greatly deceived this people and Jerusalem, saying 'You shall have peace,' whereas the sword reaches to the heart" (Jeremiah 4:10). But Jeremiah was the one who had the problem because God had repeatedly warned Judah and Jerusalem of the consequences of their sins. Any impression that God has deceived us, as believers, is due to some lack of awareness on our part, perhaps of a divine warning or a cause-and-effect relationship between some action we or others have taken and the logical outcome of the action. Or it could be we have an unrealistic view of what we deserve.

The truth of God means His interaction with us in our suffering—or His apparent lack of interaction—is rooted in the consistency of His character. Even though we are inconsistent, "He remains faithful; He cannot deny Himself" (II Timothy 2:13). The truth of God also means He does not mislead us as to the cause of our suffering. Our own surmising or the assumptions of others may mislead us, but God doesn't deceive us.

Now, let's examine the influence of God's freedom in His interaction with us in our suffering.

Freedom

In a sense, the entire Bible elaborates on Genesis 1:1. The simple statement "in the beginning God created the heavens and the earth" has profound implications. For our purposes at this point, Genesis 1:1 establishes the fact that God is distinct and independent from all He has created. He existed, uncreated, prior to all of creation. Since He is above and beyond the created realm, God does not owe His creation an explanation for His actions. He is completely free to do as He wishes. Isaiah put it this way: "Who has directed the Spirit of the Lord, or as His counselor has taught Him? With whom did He take counsel, and who instructed him, and taught Him in the path of justice? Who taught Him knowledge, and showed Him the way of understanding?" (Isaiah 40:13-14). Paul, following a discussion of the goodness of God in saving Gentiles, wrote, "Oh, the depth of the riches both of the wisdom and knowledge of God! How unsearchable are His judgments and His ways past finding out!" (Romans 11:33). Then he quoted a version of Isaiah 40:13: "For who has known the mind of the Lord? Or who has become His counselor?" (Romans 11:34).

God's freedom means He has the liberty to act without asking advice from humans, without notifying them, and without any concern for their evaluation of His actions. He doesn't seek counsel from human beings. Although He may, for His own purposes, inform humans of His plans in a specific situation, He is not obligated to do so.

As it relates to our suffering, the freedom of God means He has no responsibility to inform us that suffering is coming, to explain why it's happening as it occurs, or to answer our questions at any time in the future. Although an old gospel hymn assures us "we will understand it better by and by,"[30] God is not obligated to explain Himself to His creation.[31] This is, in part, what makes the Christian life a life of faith. We don't need faith if we can perceive with our senses. Paul wrote, "For we were saved in this hope, but hope that is seen is not hope; for why does one still hope for what he sees?" (Romans 8:24). In II Corinthians 5:7, he also wrote, "For we walk by faith, not by sight." In perhaps one of the best-known verses in the Bible, the writer of Hebrews said, "Now faith is the substance of things hoped for, the evidence of things not seen" (Hebrews 11:1). Although we will certainly see things much more clearly from an eternal perspective, we will still be created beings and God will still be the Creator. If He chooses to explain anything, that's His prerogative.

Now, let's turn our attention to how God's holiness is involved in His interaction with us in our suffering.

Holiness

To the ancient Israelites, God said, "You shall be holy; for I am holy" (Leviticus 11:44). Peter quoted this in his first letter.[32] The word "holy" has to do essentially with some kind of separation. For example, the Israelites abstained from certain kinds of food.[33] New Testament believers avoid the kind of conduct that characterized their lives before their conversion.[34] But holiness has to do not only with separation from something; it also has to do with separation unto something. In the case of biblical holiness, it has to do with separation unto God. As a consequence, believers separate themselves from all that is unlike Him.

In Genesis 1:1, the holiness of God is seen as His freedom. Since God existed before the creation, and since He exists above and beyond His creation, He is holy. He is separated unto Himself and from all that is unlike Him. In the Incarnation, God entered His creation and suffered with us.

Even here, however, His holiness was never compromised because of the miracle of the virgin birth and because Jesus was perfectly yielded to the Spirit of God. "God is light and in Him is no darkness at all" (I John 1:5).

One aspect of His holiness is that God is not contaminated by sin. He doesn't in any way "miss the mark." In both the Old and New Testaments, the most common words for sin mean "to miss the mark." They describe missing a target even by a hair's breadth. But with God, everything is precisely as it should be.

God's holiness means His involvement with us in our suffering reflects His eternal values rather than our temporal values. It also means His interaction with us is pure and untainted by darkness. God is not a sadist who inflicts pain on us for the thrill of seeing us suffer. God intends whatever suffering He may ordain or permit to help us refocus our attention on things of eternal value. Paul, who understood this, wrote, "For our light affliction, which is but for a moment, is working for us a far more exceeding and eternal weight of glory, while we do not look at the things which are seen, but at the things which are not seen. For the things which are seen are temporary, but the things which are not seen are eternal" (II Corinthians 4:17-18). In Paul's attitude toward his "thorn in the flesh," we see he really believed this principle and applied it to his own life. He said, "And lest I should be exalted above measure by the abundance of the revelations, a thorn in the flesh was given to me, a messenger of Satan to buffet me, lest I be exalted above measure. . . . Therefore most gladly I will rather boast in my infirmities, that the power of Christ may rest upon me. Therefore I take pleasure in infirmities, in reproaches, in needs, in persecutions, in distresses, for Christ's sake. For when I am weak, then I am strong" (II Corinthians 12:7-10).

57

One practical and immediate result God intends is that the experiences related to our suffering should prepare us to minister to other sufferers. Paul included this explanation in his epistle.

> Blessed be the God and Father of our Lord Jesus Christ, the Father of mercies and God of all comfort, who comforts us in all our tribulation, that we may be able to comfort those who are in any trouble, with the comfort with which we ourselves are comforted by God. For as the sufferings of Christ abound in us, so our consolation also abounds through Christ. Now if we are afflicted, it is for your consolation and salvation, which is effective for enduring the same sufferings which we also suffer. Or if we are comforted, it is for your consolation and salvation. And our hope for you is steadfast, because we know that as you are partakers of the sufferings, so also you will partake of the consolation (II Corinthians 1:3-7).

Those who respond to suffering in a way that honors God have a unique ability to identify with others in their suffering and to minister effectively to them. This certainly reflects eternal rather than earthly values.

In the following chapters, we'll consider how biblical anthropology influences the theology of suffering. What does it mean for humans to be made in the image of God? How does the image of God in man influence His interaction with us in our suffering? To what degree is our suffering a consequence of the Fall?

But for now, remember that even in the painful circumstances of life, God's justice assures us He is not abusing us, manipulating us, or in any way treating us wrongly. His truthfulness means His interaction with us in our suffering reflects the consistency of His character. He does not deceive us as to the cause of our suffering. God's freedom means He has no responsibility to inform us that suffering is coming or to explain to us now or in the future the reason for our suffering. God's holiness means He permits suffering to help us refocus on things of eternal value. Even if we're suffering due to some bad decision we've made, He still is able to comfort and strengthen us if we trust Him in the midst of our suffering.

5
Suffering and the Image of God

In previous chapters, we examined how the attributes of God influence His interaction with us in our suffering. Our study has included both incommunicable (e.g., God's omniscience means He's aware of our suffering, and God's omnipresence means He does not abandon us in our suffering) and communicable attributes (e.g., God's justice means He will not abuse us, manipulate us, or treat us wrongly; God's freedom means He does not have to tell us suffering is coming or explain to us now or in the future why we are suffering; God's holiness means He permits suffering to help us refocus on things of eternal value).

We also discovered in previous chapters that God's respect for His image in humans influences His interaction with us in our suffering. It is to this that we now turn our attention.

The Image of God in Humans

On the final day of creation, God said, "Let us make man in our image, after our likeness. . . . So God created man in his own image, in the image of God created he him; male and female created he them" (Genesis 1:26-27, KJV).

Since God created humans in His image, He relates to us as beings that bear His image. This means God cannot pretend we're something other than what we are. God relates to us the way He does, even in our suffering, as a consequence of the reality of His image in us.

What does it mean to be created in the image of God?

The human body doesn't reflect the image of God. God is an omnipresent, invisible Spirit.[35] The only body God could be said to have is in the Incarnation, and the Incarnation had not occurred at the time God created humans.[36]

The image of God in humans has to do with some kind of representation of what God is essentially like. In other words, whatever temporary manifestations of God may have occurred in the Old Testament era, humans do not replicate any one of those manifestations, for those manifestations are not what God essentially is.[37]

Essentially, God is a spirit being.[38] He's able to think, to reason, and to choose. Morally, He is sinless. God experiences the full range of emotions, from love to hatred. When God created humans, He made them to share in some way—not in His deity—but in a likeness of His essence. Thus, humans are spiritual beings who can think, reason, choose, love, and hate. They were created sinless.

In order to enable humans to live in the material realm, God also created a material body that is uniquely suited to life on earth. This material body does not reflect the image of God, for God existed before there was a material realm and even before there were other spirit beings (i.e., angels) in the immaterial realm. But God has always been what He essentially is.

The Significance of the Image
of God for Human Suffering

Humans Are Spiritual Beings

At the creation of humans, "the Lord God formed man of the dust of the ground, and breathed into his nostrils the breath of life; and man became a living being" (Genesis 2:7). Although God formed every beast and bird out of the ground,[39] man is the only creature that came into existence as God "breathed into his nostrils." Although animals also breathe, this description of the creation of man sets the tone for the entire scriptural record, which sees man as the final and highest creation in the material realm. Man is not simply another animal. He is unique on earth. His flesh is not the same as the flesh of animals, fish, or birds. Paul wrote, "All flesh is not the same flesh, but there is one kind of flesh of men, another flesh of animals, another of fish, and another of birds" (I Corinthians 15:39). And although the writer of Ecclesiastes—whose limited perspective on life was that of a man standing on earth (i.e., "under the sun")—saw a similarity between humans and animals, even he recognized that "the spirit of the sons of men . . . goes upward, and the spirit of the animal . . . goes down to the earth" (Ecclesiastes 3:21). In other words, even from the most limited, earthbound perspective, a striking difference exists between humans and animals that includes their destiny at death.

The human spirit has to do with the innermost essence of human existence.[40] It is inseparably connected in Scripture with the human soul and often seen as synonymous with the soul.[41]

Why is the fact that humans are spiritual beings significant to our study on human suffering? Any attempt to deal with human suffering as if humans were merely material beings is inadequate and misguided. Human suffering is not limited to the material realm; it reaches deep within to the recesses of the human spirit. Attempts to understand, treat, or respond to suffering on the material level are shallow and will not resolve the essential problems. Understanding, successful treatment, and informed response will come only when it's understood that humans are much more than physical beings. Although there's a place for medicine in treating human suffering, medicine alone is inadequate. Man's immaterial being must be understood and treated as well.

Humans Can Think, Reason, Choose, Love, and Hate

Like God, humans have the ability to think, reason, choose, love, and hate. Therefore, God cannot relate to us—even in our suffering—as mindless machines devoid of emotion. He cannot remove our suffering by simply giving us a "tune-up." He cannot think, reason, choose, love, and hate for us. When God created humans, He gave them the freedom to use their abilities as they wished. They could use them wisely or foolishly. They could think clearly, act reasonably, make right choices, and love and hate the things God loves and hates. But when Adam and Eve used their freedoms to rebel against God, all of their descendants were tainted with rebellion. As Paul wrote, "Therefore, just as through one man sin entered the world, and death through sin, and thus death spread to all men, because all sinned" (Romans 5:12).

Thinking and Reasoning. Since God created humans as thinking beings, we have the ability to form opinions, hold beliefs, and come to conclusions and inferences. God's respect for this aspect of His image in us is so complete that He honors our right to have opinions and beliefs, even when these opinions and beliefs are wrong. He will not force right opinions or beliefs on us.

As a consequence of the Fall, humans naturally form opinions and hold beliefs that are flawed in some measure. Satan blinds the minds of unbelievers.[42] Those who hate others walk in darkness with "blinded eyes" (I John 2:11). The negative effect of sin on our power to think is so pervasive that even after being born again, we still need the "eyes" of our understanding to be enlightened.[43]

Choosing

The Bible indicates God has the ability and freedom to make choices.[44] Isaiah prophesied the Messiah would "refuse the evil and choose the good" (Isaiah 7:14-16).

When God created humans in His image, He gave them the power of choice. This ability was not just apparent, but real. In other words, it's not that humans think they're making choices when "fate" is actually in control. If the power of choice is anything less than real, humans are not genuinely created in the image of God, for God's ability to choose is real.

The human ability to choose is seen in God's words to Adam: "Of every tree of the garden you may freely eat; but of the tree of the knowledge of good and evil you shall not eat, for in the day that you eat of it you shall surely die" (Genesis 2:16-17). Although God commanded Adam not to eat of the tree of the knowledge of good and evil, Adam made a conscious decision to do so.[45] By creating the tree of the knowledge of good and evil and placing it in the garden, God actually created an opportunity for Adam to choose wrongly. This may seem strange, but it's essential to the genuineness of the power of choice and thus to the genuineness of the divine image in humans. If humans had no opportunity to make wrong choices, they would not have real power of choice.

The human ability to choose is abundantly evident in Scripture. Humans can choose life or death.[46] They can choose whom they will worship as God.[47] God has been known to give men a choice as to what judgment He would put on them.[48] People can choose whether or not to fear the Lord.[49] People can choose one thing that is better than another. Jesus told Martha, "You are worried and troubled about many things. But one thing is needed, and Mary has chosen that good part, which will not be taken away from her" (Luke 10:41-42).

As is the case with every other aspect of the image of God in humans, the ability of humans to make choices has been marred by the influence of Adam's sin on us all.[50] All humans choose to sin.[51] Humans had the ability to sin before the Fall in Eden, but the pervasive influence of Adam's sin tilts humans so sharply in the direction of sin that the abuse of our power to choose is universal. Quoting from a variety of Old Testament texts, Paul wrote, "There is none righteous, no, not one; there is none who understands; there is none who seeks after God. They have all turned aside; they have together become unprofitable; there is none who does good, no, not one" (Romans 3:10-12).[52] This implies that much of our suffering is the result of wrong choices we or others have made. God knows when wrong choices are made, but He doesn't intervene to force the right choice upon us. To do so would demean and manipulate, indicating the image of God in man is not real.

If we choose to live wasteful, profligate lives, God will protect our freedom to do so. Such a life will certainly result in painful spiritual consequences, and it may result in physical, emotional, and mental suffering as well.

All of our choices have within them the potential of bringing painful consequences. This includes our choice of a spouse, a job, an automobile, an education . . . in short, every choice produces an incredible array of consequences. A spouse who seems kind, gentle, and thoughtful until the wedding day may turn out to be harsh, abusive, or unfaithful. The workplace may expose us to violent people or to a hazardous environment. An automobile may have a safety defect. The university campus may be unsafe, or a professor's philosophy may be deceptive and spiritually damaging.

The freedom of others to choose further complicates the potential for suffering in our own choices. Just as God will not make our choices for us, so we cannot make choices for others. If an irrational person chooses to take a weapon to his workplace with the intent of injuring others, he can do so, unless he can be physically restrained. If a violent person chooses to drive down the street shooting innocent bystanders, he can do so. Though God can and sometimes does intervene to limit suffering, He does not always do so. Since suffering is a result of sin whether as a consequence of Adam's sin or of our own choices or the choices of others, God cannot be blamed. If we blame Him, we're saying He did wrong to create us in His image. This would be a classic case of the clay saying to the Potter, "Why have you made me like this?" (Romans 9:20).

In order for us to avoid the suffering inherent in being fallen people living in a fallen world among fallen people, we would have to flee from the universe. But Jesus prayed these words, "I do not pray that You should take them out of the world, but that you should keep them from the evil one" (John 17:15).[53] We do have God's promise that Satan will not have his way with us; God will prevail. This is expressed in Jesus' promise, "In the world you will have tribulation; but be of good cheer, I have overcome the world" (John 16:33).

Our opinions and beliefs profoundly impact how we respond to suffering. Just as truth produces freedom in our lives, error produces bondage.[54] If our thoughts are wrong, we may respond to suffering in a variety of ways that contribute to bondage. Since we want to think biblically in all areas of life, including during our pain and suffering, let's review what we've learned so far:

1. Our suffering does not mean God is weak and incapable of doing good.
2. God is intimately aware of our suffering.
3. God does not abandon us in our suffering.
4. God knows what led up to our suffering and how it will conclude.
5. Our suffering is not a result of any prejudice or caprice on God's part.
6. Our suffering is not outside of God's purpose or permission.
7. Whether our suffering is a result of God's purpose or permission, He can cause it to accomplish ultimate good in our lives.
8. God will never abuse us, manipulate us, or in any way treat us wrongly.
9. God will never deceive us as to the cause of our suffering.
10. Although God may inform us suffering is coming or explain to us the reason for our suffering, He has no responsibility to do so.
11. Whether our suffering is a result of God's purpose or permission, He wants us to respond to it by refocusing our vision on things of eternal value.

If we don't think in a biblical way about our suffering, we may entertain the following errors:

1. My suffering proves either there is no God or He is so weak He can't help me.

2. God doesn't know about my pain, or He would do something about it. Therefore, I must figure out a way to make Him aware of my suffering.
3. My suffering is a sign God has abandoned me. This probably means I'm unworthy of being loved.
4. God must be as surprised as I am about my suffering.
5. My suffering proves God doesn't like me, or I have done something to prejudice Him against me.
6. My suffering proves God is not in control of the world.
7. God must be trying to humiliate me.
8. I'm suffering because God is abusing or manipulating me. Otherwise, how could He let this happen?
9. It was wrong for God not to warn me suffering was coming. It's wrong for Him not to explain to me why I'm suffering.
10. Since I'm suffering even though I put my faith in God, it doesn't do any good to trust Him.

All of these thoughts are wrong and self-defeating. Thinking this way intensifies suffering; life seems unbearable and meaningless. These beliefs contribute to despair, thoughts of suicide, or hedonism.

To a large degree, people will either endure suffering gracefully, perhaps eventually finding release from the pain of specific episodes of suffering, or their reasoning will make life seem bitter, hopeless, or meaningless.

When Paul discussed the way a believer should think, he wrote that one should think on things that are true, noble, just, pure, lovely, of good report, virtuous, and praiseworthy. The consequence of such disciplined thinking is "the God of peace will be with you" (Philippians 4:8-9).

6
Dealing with Suffering

In chapter 5, we learned that God relates to humans as beings created in His image. This means they in some way reflect, although dimly (they are, after all, only an image or likeness[55]), God's essential nature. This does not mean humans in any way share in deity; deity is unique to God. Deity cannot be created. But, like God, humans are spiritual beings capable of thinking, reasoning, choosing, loving, and hating. The material body is integral to human existence and enables humans to function in the material realm, but it's not the focus of God's imagery in humans. Humans retain the image of God even when they die, and they will be in the image of God after the resurrection, when all that is mortal about them has "put on immortality" (I Corinthians 15:42-53).

Since we're essentially spiritual beings, God's first interaction with us in our suffering is on the level of our spirit, not our body. That is, He seeks to comfort us spiritually, with assurance of His presence and His care and with the gift of inner strength. Even if we're never comforted physically, God's comfort reaches deep within to the recesses of the human spirit. Following is Paul's explanation.

Blessed be the God and Father of our Lord Jesus Christ, the Father of mercies and God of all comfort, who comforts us in all our tribulation, that we may be able to comfort those who are in any trouble, with the comfort with which we ourselves are comforted by God. For as the sufferings of Christ abound in us, so our consolation also abounds through Christ" (II Corinthians 1:3-5).[56]

Since we're created in the image of God, we can think, reason, choose, love, and hate. If we exercise these abilities in a way that honors the fact that we're created in God's image—in other words, if we use them the way God would—it will help us greatly during times of pain and suffering. But if we use these abilities in a way that's contrary to God's image in us, our pain and suffering will increase and become even more difficult.

For example, we have the ability to think, but we should think on things that are true, noble, just, pure, lovely, of good report, virtuous, and praiseworthy.[57] If we do, the God of peace will be with us.[58]72 If we think otherwise, the God of peace will remain aloof.

We have the ability to reason, but if we use that ability in a way that rules out the possibility of miracles or that tries to rationalize what cannot be explained, we are denying the very origin of our existence. We are the product of God's creative miracle, and miracles cannot be explained. God is still at work in the world, and He doesn't limit His acts to those that can be tested in a scientific laboratory. When we accept the fact that some things are beyond human explanation, we open the door to welcome God into our situation. But when we stubbornly insist we must be able to figure out all the details of life, we effectively shut God out.

So the use we make of our ability to think and reason has a profound influence on how well we endure suffering. If our thoughts are irrational—contrary to truth—they will intensify and perhaps even prolong our suffering, making it seem unbearable and making life seem meaningless. But if our thoughts harmonize with what is true about God, about the world, and about what it means to be human, we will discover the peace of God even in the midst of suffering.

We have the power of choice, one of the greatest powers known to man. But when we exercise this power, consequences follow. Foolish choices tend to produce painful consequences. Even morally neutral choices may have painful consequences, depending on how the choices of others influence us. We must recognize that the power of choice for good is at the same time the freedom to use the power of choice for evil. Also, it's apparent that since we're fallen beings, it's easier to choose evil than good.

To be made in the image of God also means we have the ability to love and hate. The Bible says a lot about God's love, but it also tells about some things God hates. How does this affect our experiences with pain and suffering?

Loving and Hating

Our ability to love and hate is connected to our ability to choose. That is, we can choose who or what we will love and hate. This is contrary to the modern idea that we can't help loving or hating. The modern Western concept of "falling in love" doesn't quite fit with the biblical idea of love as a choice. Biblically, love is not so much a feeling as it is a choice and an action.

It's possible for humans to exercise their power of choice not only to love the Lord, but also to hate Him. When God gave

Israel the Ten Commandments, He forbade them to make any carved image to worship. He said, "You shall not bow down to them nor serve them. For I, the Lord your God, am a jealous God, visiting the iniquity of the fathers upon the children to the third and fourth generations of those who hate Me, but showing mercy to thousands, to those who love Me and keep My commandments" (Exodus 20:5-6). The law of Moses warned against hating one's brother[59] or neighbors[60] or spouses.[61] Evil people can hate God's spokesmen.[62]

The ideal is, of course, for us to hate evil and love what is good.[63] This means we exercise the imagery of God in us when we love what He loves and hate what He hates. Those who love the Lord must hate evil.[64] This includes the behavior of those who turn aside from God,[65] every false way,[66] vain thoughts,[67] and lying.[68] Seven of the things God hates include pride, lying, violence, wicked plans, eagerness to participate in evil, false witness, and sowing discord among brethren.[69]

Those who love what God hates and hate what He loves will experience the painful consequences of abusing this aspect of God's image. There can be no neutrality. One way of saying it is those who hate wisdom love death.[70]

God interacts with us in our suffering as beings created in His image. This means that whether we use the aspects of His image in us wisely or whether we abuse them, God protects our right to be what we are—beings with the ability and freedom to think, reason, choose, love, and hate. He also recognizes we are primarily spiritual, not material, beings.

How Should We Respond to Suffering?

We can't avoid pain and suffering. They are consequences of the fact that we are broken people living in a broken world. This is true whether we're believers or unbelievers. Those who put their faith in Christ Jesus do not get a free pass that exempts them from the temptations experienced by all human beings. Paul wrote, "No temptation has overtaken you except such as is common to man" (I Corinthians 10:13a). The believer has the promise, however, that God in His faithfulness will not allow His children to be tempted beyond what they're able to bear. Paul continued, "God is faithful, who will not allow you to be tempted beyond what you are able, but with the temptation will also make the way of escape, that you may be able to bear it" (I Corinthians 10:13b). This does not mean a believer will never have trouble, nor does it promise an escape from every trouble. It is, rather, the promise that we will be able to bear it. He will give us the grace to endure every experience, no matter how painful. As Paul learned when God refused his request to remove his thorn in the flesh, God's grace is sufficient for us; His strength is made perfect in our weakness.[71]

It's one thing to know the promises of Scripture, but it's another to know how to respond to specific episodes of suffering. Common but self-defeating responses include denial, anger (at God, self, or others), depression, euphoria, and bargaining with God.

In order to respond to suffering in a way that honors God, we must prepare for the suffering before it comes, as it certainly will.

Dealing with Suffering

Prepare

Although it's too late to do this if the painful circumstance has already developed, the best thing to do is prepare for suffering in advance. Until we experience pain, we may live in a state of denial, thinking we'll somehow be excused from suffering.

But if we've prepared well, we can draw on the grace of God more readily and avoid unnecessary heightening of our suffering.

Preparing for suffering in advance begins with knowing that while some pain and suffering has its immediate origin in sin, this is not always the case. In the following chapters, we'll discuss suffering that is not the result of sin. For now, we'll talk about the pain and suffering that does spring from sin. But even if this is the case, we must be clear what this means. It does not mean that any specific tragedy, disease, accident, death, or any other experience of suffering is due directly to some specific sin you or others, including those who are suffering, have committed. When we experience suffering, our first question is usually why? We want to know why this happened, and we replay the event in our minds ceaselessly, trying to figure out what we could have done to avoid it. This is not helpful. Even if we did do something that caused the pain for ourselves or someone else, there's no way we can undo what has been done. In many cases, however, the thought that we caused the problem is simply not true.

Our suffering may not be rooted in any specific sin we've committed, but it may be ultimately rooted in the rebellion in Eden and in the way that rebellion has influenced the entire human race and all of creation. It's important to recognize sin as the ultimate cause of much suffering. Otherwise, we may lash out at God in our pain, when in truth not only is He not responsible for our suffering, He is the only One who can give us the strength to endure.

We must also be convinced that both God's nature and our own nature influence God's interaction with us in our suffering. Neither He nor we can be something other than what we are; we must experience life according to our nature.

As it pertains to God, we must know our suffering does

76

not signify any weakness on His part. Nor does it mean He is oblivious to our suffering or that it caught Him by surprise or that He can't tell how it may end. Our suffering does not indicate God is prejudiced against us or He is capricious. It does not mean He is not in control of the created realm.

To be best prepared, we must realize God intends every experience He ordains or permits to accomplish ultimate good in our lives. We must be convinced He would never abuse or manipulate or deceive us about the cause of our suffering.

It's essential to know God is completely free to do as He pleases and He is not obligated to notify us in advance that suffering is coming or explain the reason for our suffering. He may choose to do one or the other of these things, but He has no obligation to do so.

God intends that our suffering will help us refocus our vision on things of eternal value.

As it pertains to our nature, we must recognize God honors His image in us to the point that He will not override our free exercise of that image, which includes our inherent spirit nature, our ability to think, reason, choose, love, and hate. Whatever the consequences of our use of His image, we must face them. God's first effort to comfort us in our suffering will be in the realm of our spirit, where our essential identity resides.

Grieve

Not only must we prepare for suffering before it comes, we must recognize when suffering does come that grief is a gift from God to help us begin the process of emotional healing. As Solomon said, "There is a time to weep . . . and a time to mourn" (Ecclesiastes 3:4). Upon the death of Stephen, those who were devout "made great lamentation over him" (Acts 8:2). Because our first reaction to tragedy tends to be

77

shock—a kind of numbing of the emotions—we may mistakenly think we or others are handling pain with great strength when in fact the reality of the tragedy has not yet settled upon us. Tears are a marvelous aid to healing.

First-century Jews valued the grief process so highly they commonly hired mourners to help them grieve. We tend to mock this practice as hypocritical, but it's no more hypocritical than the common practice of hiring musicians and singers to help us celebrate our joy at a wedding.

Believers should embrace sorrow as a friend, but our sorrow is tempered by our hope of a future free from pain.[72]

After the shock of tragedy, it's not unusual for people to move to denial. Although it's irrational, it's not uncommon for people to think if they refuse to accept the tragic circumstance as real, it will go away.

When it is clear that denial will not erase the pain, sufferers move from denial to anger. This anger may be directed inwardly ("Why did I let this happen?" or "If only . . .") or outwardly (at God or at the persons [even the victims] involved in the event that produced the pain).

A possible form of denial is euphoria. In this case, a sufferer may deny any sense of grief or pain and may behave irrationally.

Sometimes those who are suffering bargain with God. They may make all kinds of promises in an attempt to "deal" with God so He will take away the cause of the suffering.

It's possible that those who are suffering may sink into deep depression. They may be captivated by a morose sense of helplessness, a blue mood.

To grieve properly, we must accept the reality of our suffering and own our pain. Tears are a sign of emotional strength, not weakness.

Accept

Some people are tempted to rush through the grief process, but we must come to accept the reality of our loss. We must move away from "what if," "if only," and "why" to "what now?"[73]

As a consequence of David's sin with Bathsheba, Nathan told David, "Because by this deed you have given great occasion to the enemies of the Lord to blaspheme, the child also who is born to you shall surely die" (II Samuel 12:14). David responded by pleading with God for the child, fasting at night while he lay on the ground, and refusing to eat. This went on for seven days, until David's servants were afraid to tell him that in spite of all he had done, the child had died. They said, "Indeed, while the child was alive, we spoke to him, and he would not heed our voice. How can we tell him that the child is dead? He may do some harm!" (II Samuel 12:18). When David learned the child was dead, he arose from the ground, washed and anointed himself, changed his clothes, went into the house of the Lord, and worshiped. Then he went to his own house and requested food. David's servants said, "What is this you have done? You fasted and wept for the child while he was alive, but when the child died, you arose and ate food" (II Samuel 12:21). David replied, "While the child was alive, I fasted and wept; for I said, 'Who can tell whether the Lord will be gracious to me, that the child may live?' But now he is dead; why should I fast? Can I bring him back again? I shall go to him, but he shall not return to me" (II Samuel 12:22-23).

When he first heard the news that his child would die, David began the grieving process while hoping the Lord would change His mind. But when he saw this was not to be, he accepted his loss and took steps to move on with life. This may at first seem cold and unfeeling, but it's the only way to deal with the reality of loss. If we become mired in grief, we never fully honor our loss by recognizing that life will never be the same. If, however, we realistically reassess our future under these changed circumstances, we will be able to move past the grief.

Trust

Not only must we prepare for suffering and grieve and accept our loss, we must put our trust in God. David sang, "Whenever I am afraid, I will trust in you" (Psalm 56:3). Some suggest that believers should never admit to any negative emotion, including fear. David confessed his fear, but he did not become mired in fear. Instead, his fear prompted him to trust in God.

Trust in God is made meaningful when we cast ourselves on the mercies of God even when we do not understand our circumstances. In other words, trust does not demand an explanation.

Trust involves prayer. If we trust God, we will communicate with Him. Paul wrote, "Be anxious for nothing, but in everything by prayer and supplication, with thanksgiving, let your requests be made known to God; and the peace of God, which surpasses all understanding, will guard your hearts and minds through Christ Jesus" (Philippians 4:6-7). Instead of being captured by anxiety, we talk to God about everything and tell Him our requests. When we're honest with God, His peace, which surpasses all understanding, can guard our hearts and minds. Knowing everything about our suffering does not bring peace; it is brought because we trust God in the midst of our suffering. This peace is not linked to understanding.

Share

Another important response to suffering is to share with others what we're going through. An old maxim declares, "Joy shared is a joy doubled; a sorrow shared is a sorrow halved." Sharing your pain with those who care is therapeutic. Paul wrote that Christians are to practice empathy: "Rejoice with those who rejoice, and weep with those who weep" (Romans 12:15). But in order for others to share your pain, you must be willing to let them do so.

Others can bring great comfort to you just by their presence. They will probably not know what to say, and they may even say things that are not helpful in their attempt to minister to you. But knowing that others care enough to be with you in your suffering promotes emotional healing. Even Jesus wanted His closest disciples with Him in His agony.[74]

With the passing of time, you must allow others to help you process your feelings. Although others can help you, you also must be willing to find and internalize your own answers from Scripture.

Look for the Good

Finally, it should be noted that when we first encounter an episode of suffering, we'll probably not be able to see any good in it or how any good could come from it. It would probably be counterproductive to respond initially to suffering by saying, "Surely there must be some good reason for this!" It would probably not help at that time for others to quote Romans 8:28 to us. In fact, this approach would probably drive us farther into despair because we have not had time to grieve and to process our emotions.

But from the perspective of time—sometimes years— you will probably be able to see how God has worked either through or in spite of your pain to bring about something good. It may not always be that you will see any good come from your suffering in this life, but many people have discovered, looking back on their suffering, that God found a way to bring something good out of what seemed at the moment to be unbearable.

In chapter 7, we'll examine the apparent prosperity of the wicked while the righteous suffer, and we'll discover a point of view that will help us come to grips with this problem and gain a better grasp on reality.

7
Why Don't the Wicked Suffer?

As we noted in chapter 6, some pain and suffering is the direct or indirect result of sin. It's impossible to sin with impunity, although the Bible does discuss the apparent prosperity of the wicked. Asaph recorded his struggle with this in one of his psalms.

Truly God is good to Israel, to such as are pure in heart. But as for me, my feet had almost stumbled; my steps had nearly slipped. For I was envious of the boastful, when I saw the prosperity of the wicked. For there are no pangs in their death, but their strength is firm. They are not in trouble as other men, nor are they plagued like other men. Therefore pride serves as their necklace; violence covers them like a garment. Their eyes bulge with abundance; they have more than heart could wish. They scoff and speak wickedly concerning oppression; they speak loftily. They set their mouth against the heavens, and their tongue walks through the earth. Therefore his people return here and waters of a full cup are drained by them. And they say, "How does God know? And is there knowledge in the Most High?" Behold, these are the ungodly, who are always at ease; they increase in riches. Surely I have cleansed my heart in vain, and washed my hands in innocence. For all day long I have been plagued, and chastened every morning (Psalm 73:1-14).

Can you identify with Asaph? Have you ever wondered why the wicked prosper? Why do things seem to go so well for them, when you've tried to do right and yet have all kinds of problems? Does God even know what's going on? Is it pointless to try to live right? These were Asaph's questions, and they're questions many of us have.

But Asaph's psalm doesn't end there. He thought further about the problem, and this helped him to see beyond the obvious.

If I had said, "I will speak thus," behold, I would have been untrue to the generation of Your children. When I thought how to understand this, it was too painful for me—until I went into the sanctuary of God; then I understood their end. Surely You set them in slippery places; You cast them down to destruction. Oh, how they are brought to desolation, as in a moment! They are utterly consumed with terrors (Psalm 73:15-19).

By looking only at what was visible in the temporal realm, Asaph didn't get a clear picture of reality. It looked like there was no point in serving God; the wicked were doing much better than the righteous. They prospered and they didn't experience trouble like the righteous even though they were proud, violent, and oppressive. They spoke against God and died apparently peaceful deaths.

It was not until he went into the sanctuary of God that Asaph's vision cleared. When he saw the situation as God saw it, Asaph understood the end of the wicked. From this new perspective, Asaph said, "Surely You set them in slippery places; You cast them down to destruction. Oh, how they are brought to desolation, as in a moment! They are utterly consumed with terrors" (Psalm 73:18-19).

The idea that the wicked prosper is deceptive because it's a one-dimensional view. The apparent prosperity of those who reject God comes from looking only at the visible, temporary things. This doesn't take the invisible world into account; it doesn't take eternity into account. Paul wrote, "For our light affliction, which is but for a moment, is working for us a far more exceeding and eternal weight of glory, while we do not look at the things which are seen, but at the things which are not seen. For the things which are seen are temporary, but the things which are not seen are eternal" (II Corinthians 4:17-18).

Moses could endure the loss of privilege and status in Egypt because he saw "Him who is invisible" (Hebrews 11:27). Had Moses looked only at what he could see with his natural eyes—if he hadn't looked to the future—he wouldn't have had the courage to do what he did. If he had looked only at the visible circumstances, he would never have been able to lead the people of Israel from the bondage of their humiliating and painful suffering.

Many of the people of faith listed in Hebrews 11 died without having received the promises, but they saw them "afar off" (Hebrews 11:13). As long as we look only at what can be seen with our natural eyes, we'll be deceived into thinking there's really no point in trusting God, because the wicked prosper and we suffer. But this view leaves the future out of the picture, both for those who trust God and those who don't.

This can be seen in two back-to-back verses in Psalm 37. This psalm is especially interesting because David wrote it in the form of an acrostic. In the original Hebrew of the psalm, verse 1 starts with the first letter of the Hebrew alaphabet, alpha. The third verse begins with the second letter, beth. The fifth verse begins with the third letter, gimel, and so forth, until we get to verse 37, which begins with the letter shin. But before we look at the content of the two verses marked by shin, let's notice what the psalm says about the prosperity of the wicked and how illusory it is.

Psalm 37 provides a major advance on the Psalter's theme of the contrast between the righteous and the wicked, a contrast that begins in Psalm 1. As this theme is developed in Psalm 2, the wicked are those who reject the Messiah; the righteous are those who trust in the Messiah. It could be said that the central themes of Psalms 1-2 and of the entire Psalter are restated in Psalm 37.[75] The messianic significance of Psalm 37 is seen in the connection between Psalm 2:4 and Psalm 37:13.

"He who sits in the heavens shall laugh; the Lord shall hold them in derision" (Psalm 2:4).

"The Lord laughs at him, for He sees that his day is coming" (Psalm 37:13).

In these verses, as well as in the context that surrounds them in both psalms, there's a connection that ties Psalm 37 together with all of the previous messianic psalms. This connection may also be seen by comparing Psalm 2:12 with Psalm 37:40.

"Kiss the Son, lest He be angry, and you perish in the way, when his wrath is kindled but a little. Blessed are all those who put their trust in Him" (Psalm 2:12).

"And the Lord shall help them and deliver them; He shall deliver them from the wicked, and save them, because they trust in Him" (Psalm 37:40).

In both psalms, the way to deliverance is the way of trusting in the Messiah.

Another evidence that Psalm 37 is intentionally placed and that it seamlessly advances the messianic theme of the Psalter may be seen by comparing the last verse of Psalm 36 and the first two verses of Psalm 37.

"There the workers of iniquity have fallen; they have been cast down and are not able to rise" (Psalm 36:12).

"Do not fret because of evildoers, nor be envious of the workers of iniquity. For they shall soon be cut down like the grass, and wither as the green herb" (Psalm 37:1-2).

Psalm 36 concludes with a discussion of the workers of iniquity, whereas Psalm 37 begins with a similar discussion. Psalm 36 concludes by saying that the workers of iniquity have been cast down, and Psalm 37 begins by saying the workers of iniquity will soon be cut down. Psalm 36 concludes by saying the workers of iniquity are not able to rise; Psalm 37 begins by saying the workers of iniquity will wither as the green herb. Thematically, these psalms are one. Since Psalm 36 advances the messianic theme of the Psalter, so must Psalm 37. Although we don't know when David originally wrote either psalm, as they're placed in the Psalter in this intentional arrangement, they're intended to be read as a flowing, uninterrupted progression of thought.

As we've mentioned, Psalm 37 is an acrostic, which indicates an intentional arrangement of the verses to advance a specific theme. In this case, that theme is the contrast between the wicked and the righteous. In the Hebrew text, the acrostic begins with verse 1 and continues with every other line to verse 39, with one exception. There are two lines between the lines that begin with the adjoining letters heth and teth. The extra line here appears as verse 15 in our English translations: "Their sword shall enter their own heart, and their bows shall be broken." When the acrostic is interrupted in this way, it's for emphasis. Attention is directed to the point where the acrostic is irregular, somewhat like underlining or highlighting. In this case, the psalm calls attention to the destruction of the wicked. They will experience the destruction they're attempting to perpetrate upon the righteous. This connects Psalm 37 with Psalm 7. Psalm 7, which concludes the section of the Psalter that begins in Psalm 3 and describes Absalom's rebellion, says concerning the wicked, "His trouble shall return upon his own head, and his violent dealing shall come down on his own crown" (Psalm 7:16). The section of the Psalter dealing with the rebellion of Absalom describes the first attempt to thwart God's messianic purpose. God had promised David that the Messiah would descend from Him, not from Absalom.[76] Absalom's plot failed. The connection of Psalm 37 with Psalm 7 indicates that all such plots will fail. Absalom was not the only wicked person who would attempt to thwart God's promise. There would be many others who would try in a variety of ways to defeat the divinely ordained plan. None would succeed. These vain attempts continued right up to the efforts of Herod to assassinate the boy Jesus. But the good news of the Psalter is that although the wicked may rise up, they will not prevail.

In Psalm 37, the wicked (rasha) are specifically mentioned in thirteen verses.[77] The righteous (tsadiq) are specifically mentioned in ten verses.[78] The wicked are implied, but not specifically mentioned, in seven verses.[79] The righteous are implied, but not specifically mentioned, in twenty-one verses.[80] There are four verses where the wicked and the righteous are specifically mentioned in the same verse.[81] There are four verses where the wicked are specifically mentioned and the righteous are implied in the same verse.[82]

Psalm 37 appears to be structured as follows: Verses 1-11 show "the need for patience in light of the apparent success of the wicked"; verses 12-22 show "the need for patience in light of the final judgment of the wicked"; verses 23-33 provide "encouragement for the righteous in view of the role of the wicked"; verses 34-40 give "a renewed call for patience in view of the apparent success of the wicked."[83]

Be Patient: The Success of the Wicked Is Only Apparent (Psalm 37:1-11)

Those who trust in the Lord (see verse 3) are not to worry because of those who do evil, nor are they to envy those who work iniquity (verse 1). The reason for this is that the doom of evildoers is certain (verse 2).

The antidote to worrying about those who do evil is to trust in the Lord, to do what is right, to dwell in the land promised to the patriarchs (by application, this means believers should receive and enjoy God's promises), to be strengthened by God's faithfulness (verse 3), to delight oneself in the Lord (verse 4), to commit one's ways to Him (verse 5), to rest in Him, to wait patiently for Him (verse 7), to cease from anger, and to forsake wrath (verse 8). The reward for this is that the Lord will give those who trust in Him the desires of their heart (verses 4-5).

He will demonstrate to all that they're in the right standing with Him; He will see that justice is done for them (verse 6).

Although it may seem the wicked are prospering and they're getting their way (verse 7), they will be "cut off" (verse 9). But those who wait on the Lord will "inherit the earth" (verse 9). That is, they will fully enjoy the promises God has given to them. For the people of Israel, this was connected with the land, the earth, and the promise to Abraham, Isaac, and Jacob.

It will not be long before the wicked cannot be found (verse 10). But the meek can be found, for they will inherit the earth and "delight themselves in the abundance of peace" (verse 11). Jesus quoted this verse in the Sermon on the Mount.[84]

Be Patient: The Wicked Will Be Judged (Psalm 37:12-22)

Although the wicked plot against the righteous (verse 12), their efforts will not succeed because the Lord laughs at their plans in view of their day of judgment (verse 13).[85] When the wicked attempt to destroy the upright, the poor, and the needy, they seal their own doom (verses 14-15). Though a righteous man may have little, it's better than the riches of the wicked (verse 16). The Lord sides with the righteous; He opposes the wicked (verse 17). The upright have an eternal inheritance (verse 18). Their trust in God will not be disappointed even in bad times (verse 19). The wicked, on the other hand, will perish like the fading splendor of the meadows or like vanishing smoke (verse 20). The wicked are characterized by their refusal to pay what they owe; the righteous are characterized by showing mercy and by generosity (verse 21). The righteous will receive the promise of God; the wicked will be cut off (verse 22).

Be Encouraged: The Lord Is for the Righteous (Psalm 37:23-33)

The Lord directs the steps of good people; He delights in the way of the righteous (verse 23).[86] A righteous man may fall, but the Lord will help him rise (verse 24). This is not the case with the wicked; when they fall, they're unable to rise.[87] At no time had David seen the righteous forsaken by God; he had never seen their descendants begging bread (verse 25). The reason for this is that God is a merciful, generous God who blesses the descendants of the righteous (verse 26).

In order to be righteous, one must depart from evil and do what's right. If one does this, he'll be able to dwell permanently in the land promised to Abraham, Isaac, and Jacob (verse 27).[88]

The Lord will see that justice is done for those who trust Him (His saints); He will not forsake them (verse 28).[89] The Lord will preserve His saints, just as surely as the descendants of the wicked will be cut off (verse 28). The righteous will inherit the land and dwell in it permanently (verse 29).[90]

The words of the righteous are characterized by wisdom and justice (verse 30). This is because "the law of his God is in his heart" (verse 31).[91] As a consequence, "None of his steps shall slide" (verse 31).

Although the wicked look for opportunities to slay the righteous (verse 32), the Lord will not abandon the righteous into the hand of the wicked (verse 33). When the righteous are judged by the wicked, the Lord will not join the wicked in their condemnation (verse 33).

Be Patient: The Lord Will Keep His Promises (Psalm 37:34-40)

The righteous wait on the Lord and keep His way (verse 34). The concept of life as a "way" links Psalm 37 with a theme that begins in Psalm 1:1. The Hebrew *derek*, translated "way," takes a very practical view of life; it's a way of living. The way of the wicked contrasts with the way the righteous. The Lord exalts those who keep His way by giving them as their inheritance the land promised to Abraham, Isaac, and Jacob (verse 34). The righteous will also see it when the wicked are cut off (verse 34).

The wicked are sometimes perceived to prosper (verse 35), yet their prosperity is temporary (verse 36).

The Lord promises peace to the blameless and upright (verse 37), but transgressors will be destroyed (verse 38).

The Lord delivers the righteous; He will strengthen them during troubling times (verse 39). Specifically, He will deliver them from the wicked (verse 40). The Lord delivers the righteous because they trust in Him (verse 40). This concluding verse ties Psalm 37 together with the theme of trust in the Messiah, a theme beginning in Psalm 2:12.[92]

So the next-to-the-last two verses in Psalm 37, the verses marked by the next-to-the-last letter in the Hebrew alphabet, are concerned with the future of the righteous and the wicked: "Mark the blameless man, and observe the upright; for the future of that man is peace. But the transgressors shall be destroyed together; the future of the wicked shall be cut off" (Psalm 37:37-38). When we look only at what we can see at this moment, it may seem there is no advantage to doing right and that the wicked are doing well. But when we look to the future, we see that for those who do right, the future is peace; on the other hand, the future of the wicked is to be cut off.

When we experience loss, disappointment, pain, and suffering, we may think we have come to the end of our world. We may entertain thoughts of running away, thinking things will be different elsewhere. We often feel we've failed and our best days are behind us. But some of the most amazing words in Scripture are those God spoke to the ancient Israelite captives in Babylon. In this case, their suffering was their own fault. They had sinned against God with such persistence and severity that they had lost everything: homes, wealth, the land God had promised them, and even the magnificent Temple built by Solomon. But in the midst of their suffering, God promised them a favorable future.

> For I know the thoughts that I think toward you, says the Lord, thoughts of peace and not of evil, to give you a future and a hope. Then you will call upon Me and go and pray to Me, and I will listen to you. And you will seek Me and find Me, when you search for Me with all your heart. I will be found by you, says the Lord, and I will bring you back from your captivity (Jeremiah 29:11-14).

Although these words were spoken to the ancient Israelites, they have a wonderful application for us today. We may feel we've lost it all. Perhaps we are responsible for bringing our troubles on ourselves. But even if that's true, God's thoughts toward us are thoughts of peace, not of evil. He wants the best for us. He doesn't want to see us suffer. He wants to give us a hopeful future. God knows that a life without hope is a life of aimlessness and misery. The right response to our suffering is to call upon our Lord and pray to Him. If we do, He has promised to listen. When we seek for Him with all of our heart, we will find Him.

Don't fall for the deception that the wicked are prosperous and free of pain. Take the longer view. Realize that today is not all there is. A glorious, peaceful future awaits for all of those who will turn to God in the midst of their suffering.

8
Suffering, Sin, Time, and Chance

It's true: the Bible teaches that some suffering, even for Christians, is associated with sin. In his first letter to the church at Corinth, a letter characterized largely by Paul's attempts to correct a variety of sins among the believers, Paul dealt with the problem of their abuse of the Lord's Supper. Instead of recognizing this was an event to commemorate the death of Jesus, some of the people were dividing into factions, preferring themselves over others, and even getting drunk during this holy event. Paul said, "What! Do you not have houses to eat and drink in? Or do you despise the church of God and shame those who have nothing? What shall I say to you? Shall I praise you in this? I do not praise you" (I Corinthians 11:22).

After explaining the true purpose for the Lord's Supper, Paul continued, "Therefore whoever eats this bread or drinks this cup of the Lord in an unworthy manner will be guilty of the body and blood of the Lord. But let a man examine himself, and so let him eat of the bread and drink of the cup. For he who eats and drinks in an unworthy manner eats and drinks judgment to himself, not discerning the Lord's body" (I Corinthians 11:27-29).

Notice that these people professed to be Christians. They were celebrating the Lord's Supper, although in a way that contradicted the core meaning of the supper. Paul warned of the penalty for this: "For this reason many are weak and sick among you, and many sleep. For if we would judge ourselves, we would not be judged. But when we are judged, we are chastened by the Lord, that we may not be condemned with the world" (I Corinthians 11:30-33). As we consider the problem of suffering, some important insights arise from this text. First, if we abuse God's good gifts, we will experience the penalty for our sin. Like the Corinthians, we may experience weakness, sickness, or even premature death. If our suffering is due to our sin, there's no point in getting angry at God. The solution to our problem is not to rail against God or anyone else, but, as Paul said, to judge ourselves.

Now I don't want you to jump immediately to the conclusion that if something is going wrong in your life, it's because of some specific sin in your life. You can go down the road of introspection only so far. At some point, you must quit examining and reexamining yourself or you will wind up in despair. If your suffering is directly due to sin, you will know it without having to plumb the depths of your psyche. The judgment that had come on the Corinthians was not because of subtle sins that could be identified only by intensive examination. Their sins were quite obvious. They were proud, arrogant, selfish, and intoxicated! I want to make this point clear, because many times honest people will spend huge amounts of time and energy trying to figure out what they've done wrong to merit their suffering, when they've done nothing at all.

The second insight to be gained from the Corinthians' situation is both startling and comforting. Even though God chastened them with weakness, sickness, and premature death, it was so they would not be condemned along with the world. In other words, although their suffering was painful, God intended it for their good. He chastened them because He loved them, even though they were abusing the sacred celebration of the Lord's Supper. Condemnation is judgment. In order to prevent the Corinthians from being condemned, or judged, with unbelievers, a judgment that can lead only to eternal suffering, God judged them as part of the believing community with a disciplinary judgment that was intended to restore them to fellowship with Him. The good news here is this: God judges sinning believers in a special way intended to lead to restoration; He disciplines them as His children. One of the clearest explanations of this is found in Hebrews 12:5-11.

And you have forgotten the exhortation which speaks to you as to sons: "My son, do not despise the chastening of the Lord, nor be discouraged when you are rebuked by Him; for whom the Lord loves He chastens, and scourges every son whom He receives." If you endure chastening, God deals with you as with sons; for what son is there whom a father does not chasten? But if you are without chastening, of which all have become partakers, then you are illegitimate and not sons. Furthermore, we have had human fathers who corrected us, and we paid them respect. Shall we not much more readily be in subjection to the Father of spirits and live? For they indeed for a few days chastened us as seemed best to them, but He for our profit, that we may be partakers of His holiness. Now no chastening seems to be joyful for the present, but painful; nevertheless, afterward it yields the peaceable fruit of righteousness to those who have been trained by it.

This text offers such rich insight for the suffering Christian! First, it's addressed to believers, specifically Hebrew Christians who were apparently reconsidering their commitment to Jesus Christ. Their pain and suffering was due to God's chastening because of their need for correction. Second, the text reveals how even the Old Testament Scriptures continue to speak to New Testament believers. The quote introduced by the phrase "the exhortation which speaks to you," is from the Book of Proverbs. The present tense form of the verb shows that the Book of Proverbs consists not just of ancient wisdom for people of the past, but it continues to offer a current message for all who believe. In this case, it's a message of correction, a warning not to despise the chastening of the Lord and not to be discouraged by His rebuke. Chastening is a sign of God's love, for He scourges every son whom He receives. The text uses the analogy of human fathers who chasten their sons when they need correction.

The third point is shown by this analogy: If we respected our human fathers in their corrective efforts, we should certainly accept the chastening of the Father of spirits. Accepting His chastening leads us to life. Fourth, God chastens us for our profit so we can partake of His holiness. Fifth, the text points out that although no one enjoys the pain of chastening, it produces peace for those who accept the training God intends.

Again, remember that not all suffering—by any means—is chastisement from God for believers' sins. But we wouldn't do justice to our attempt to gain a biblical perspective on suffering if we didn't note that, in some cases, suffering is precisely due to God's chastening. If it is, our response must be to accept the correction and turn from our sins.

James addressed this issue quite early in the first century.

Is anyone among you suffering? Let him pray. Is anyone cheerful? Let him sing psalms. Is anyone among you sick? Let him call for the elders of the church, and let them pray over him, anointing him with oil in the name of the Lord. And the prayer of faith will save the sick, and the Lord will raise him up. And if he has committed sins, he will be forgiven. Confess your trespasses to one another, and pray for one another, that you may be healed. The effective, fervent prayer of a righteous man avails much (James 5:13-16).

Notice here the possibility that believers will suffer. The proper response to suffering is to pray, or to talk to God about your pain. It's quite interesting that this reference to suffering is found in the context of sickness, especially sickness that may be due to sin, like the sickness of the Corinthian believers. I must quickly say there is no hint in Scripture that sickness is always or even frequently due to sin committed by the suffering person. But again, it's clear this is sometimes the case. James may mean here that if a believer is suffering with a sickness due to unconfessed sin, he should call for the elders of the church to pray over him and anoint him with oil in the name of the Lord. When the prayer of faith is prayed, the Lord will raise up this sick person and, at the same time, forgive that person's sins, apparently the sins that caused the sickness. That this is the case is further suggested by the next words of the text, which tell us we should confess our trespasses and pray for one another in order to be healed.

Still further evidence that James is examining the same kind of disciplinary chastening seen in I Corinthians and Hebrews is found immediately after his brief reference to the faith of Elijah. He wrote, "Brethren, if anyone among you wanders from the truth, and someone turns him back, let him know that he who turns a sinner from the error of his way will save a soul from death and cover a multitude of sins" (James 5:19-20). Here is a brother who has wandered from the truth. God is so concerned that this person be saved He will, if need be, chasten him. Those who minister to this person in his sickness are responsible for turning him from death and saving his soul.

It's probably important to point out that the words "confess your trespasses to one another" do not encourage open, indiscriminate public confession of one's personal sins.

> The passage addresses a specific, limited situation in which certain negative spiritual or physical consequences have resulted from sin; the recovery is aided by the confession of these sins—not to the church at large, but to the spiritual leaders, the elders, who are offering prayer. Alternatively, the verse may mean confession to a fellow Christian . . . of a wrong done to him.[93]

The possible connection between personal sins and sickness is seen in some of the miracles of Jesus. In one of these accounts, Jesus healed a man who was paralyzed because of some personal sin.

> So He got into a boat, crossed over, and came to His own city. Then behold, they brought to Him a paralytic lying on a bed. When Jesus saw their faith, He said to the paralytic, "Son, be of good cheer; your sins are forgiven you." And at once some of the scribes said within themselves, "This Man blasphemes!" But Jesus, knowing their thoughts, said, "Why do you think evil in your hearts? For which is easier to say, 'Your sins are forgiven you,' or to say, 'Arise and walk'? But that you may know that the Son of Man has power on earth to forgive sins"—then

He said to the paralytic, "Arise, take up your bed, and go to your house" (Matthew 9:1-6).

It seems quite clear that, like the sick person in James, there was a connection between this man's paralysis and his sins. Whether Jesus said, "Your sins are forgiven," or, "Arise and walk," the effect was the same. If Jesus said, "Your sins are forgiven," the man would be healed because his sickness was due to his sins. If Jesus said, "Arise and walk," the man's sins would be forgiven, for his inability to walk was due to his sins. This is why Jesus asked, "Which is easier to say?"

On another occasion, at the Pool of Bethesda, Jesus healed a man who had suffered with an infirmity for thirty-eight years. This story is quite well-known because it's the occasion when Jesus told the man to take up his bed and walk, even though it was the Sabbath day. When Jesus saw this man later in the Temple, He said to the man, "See, you have been made well. Sin no more, lest a worse thing come upon you" (John 5:14). Apparently, this man's infirmity was due to some personal sin. Although the text doesn't tell us, the connection between his healing and the forgiveness of his sins seems evident. This is the point of Jesus' warning.

We've discussed possible connections between suffering and sin. Although I was somewhat reluctant to do this, it had to be done in order to gain a full view of what Scripture says on the subject of suffering. The reason I hesitated is that one of the first things believers do when suffering comes is to ask themselves, "What have I done wrong? Is God punishing me? What sin have I committed?" This kind of introspection can spiral out of control as we search for sin in our lives to explain our suffering. Later we'll look carefully at the story of Job, but just a quick glance at Job's suffering shows there is no necessary connection between our suffering and any sin we've committed. Suffering has many causes—we'll talk about several—but sin is only one of them. For now, keep this in mind: If your suffering is due to some sin in your life, you'll know it without intense self-examination. The biblical witness seems to be that God uses suffering to chasten His children only when every other effort to correct them has failed, including the corrective influence of Scripture, the efforts of pastors and teachers, and the voice of the Holy Spirit. By the time God must resort to the chastisement of suffering, one's sin will be so blatant and obvious that no guesswork will be needed to identify it. Remember the blatant sins of the Corinthians.

And now we come to one of the most important, yet mystifying, teachings of Scripture on the subject of suffering. Much of the suffering we experience is simply unexplained and unexplainable. Solomon said many things that happen are due to time and chance.

> The race is not to the swift, nor the battle to the strong, nor bread to the wise, nor riches to men of understanding, nor favor to men of skill; but time and chance happen to them all. For man also does not know his time: like fish taken in a cruel net, like birds caught in a snare, so the sons of men are snared in an evil time, when it falls suddenly upon them (Ecclesiastes 9:11-12).

If everything that happens in life is predestined, if there is such a thing as fate, how could there be any possibility of chance? Read this text in the New Living Translation.

> I have observed something else in this world of ours. The fastest runner doesn't always win the race, and the stron-

gest warrior doesn't always win the battle. The wise are often poor, and the skillful are not necessarily wealthy. And those who are educated don't always lead success-ful lives. It is all decided by chance, by being at the right place at the right time. People can never predict when hard times might come. Like fish in a net or birds in a snare, people are often caught by sudden tragedy.

Those of us who believe the Bible is God's Word to human-ity want to be able to embrace and affirm everything that's written within its pages. But to be candid, something doesn't sound quite right about this. If there is a God, and if He has any influence at all on what will happen in the future, how can it be said that "it is all decided by chance"? We'll talk about the Book of Ecclesiastes later, along with the Books of Job and Proverbs, but for now, notice we didn't read the important introduction to this text. Here are the first words of Ecclesiastes 9:11: "I returned and saw under the sun that . . ." The phrase "under the sun" appears twenty-seven times in the Book of Ecclesiastes. This is quite significant, for it reveals the overall perspective of the book. While many books of the Bible give us the view of life from God's eternal perspective or from Heaven, Ecclesiastes offers the view of life from the per-spective of those who stand on planet earth: under the sun. In other words, when you're looking at life from a merely human and earthbound view, this is what seems to be true. From this earthly view, it looks like if you're a runner, there's no advan-tage to being swift. In battle, the strong have no advantage. In the search for food, it doesn't help to be wise. Understanding is no benefit in the attempt to earn money. The reason for this is that time and chance interrupt all of human life. By chance, the fast runner may stumble and fall. By chance, the weaker army may outwit the stronger army. Regardless of how wise a person may be, he may be no more able in a time of famine to find food than anyone else. Those who seek to earn money may find there is no demand for their field of expertise. These are just some initial thoughts. But the point is, it seems that time and chance win out in the end. As the New Living Translation puts it, a great deal depends on being in the right place at the right time. And, we could add, a lot of suffering is the result of being in the wrong place at the wrong time. As the next verse in Ecclesiastes puts it, "People can never predict when hard times might come. Like fish in a net or birds in a snare, people are often caught by sudden tragedy."

Recently, my wife and I saw the truth of this lesson. About eight inches of snow had just blanketed our community. I had shoveled our sidewalk and driveway twice, and we had been able to get out and about as needed. The roads were clear. On the day I'm telling you about, the weather was quite nice, but cold. Judy decided to walk out to the mailbox, and I went to my office, which is located in the front of our home. I can see the mailbox from my office window. Shortly after I sat down at my computer, I heard Judy's voice calling weakly, "Dan!" Looking out the window, I saw her lying on the driveway, letters still clutched in her hand.

How quickly and unexpectedly these things can happen! Judy had slipped on a patch of ice and, almost instantly and without any time to think, fell backwards and hit her head hard on the concrete. She was disoriented, dizzy, and in pain. After I got her into the house, we discovered a large lump about the size of half an orange on the back of her head. The CAT scan in the hospital emergency room revealed there was no internal injury or damage to her skull, for which we're extremely thankful to God. Things could have been much worse. But things like these seem to happen, as Solomon observed, by chance. We call them accidents. Judy certainly didn't plan to slip and fall. Scripture does not require me to believe God planned and executed her fall.

Even Jesus believed in chance. In His parable of the Good Samaritan, after Jesus described how the thieves attacked the man who was going down from Jerusalem to Jericho, He said, "Now by chance a certain priest came down that road. And when he saw him, he passed by on the other side" (Luke 10:31).

The word "chance" means "the absence of any known reason why an event should turn out one way rather than another."[94] Since Jesus Himself used this word, we shouldn't fear to use it. We may be wrong about some things we think have happened according to chance. There may be a reason after all, and we may discover what it is some day. But there will be many events in life, some of which will bring pain and suffering, for which we will never know the reason. In order to have peace in our hearts, we must believe God is worthy of being trusted both when we know why certain events have occurred and when we don't know the reason.

The fact there's such a thing as chance doesn't mean God isn't in control or that He doesn't know what will happen in the future. It just means He doesn't micromanage the universe. Since we're human beings made in His image, He gives us freedom of choice. Since every person has this freedom, our interaction with each other as well as our involvement with the entire realm of creation often produces results we didn't anticipate. These results are often pleasant, but they can also be painful. A great deal of suffering is the result of what we would call chance events, or accidents.

When we think about chance events and the uncertainty of life, these words of Jesus can comfort us: "Are not two sparrows

105

sold for a copper coin? And not one of them falls to the ground apart from your Father's will. But the very hairs of your head are all numbered. Do not fear therefore; you are of more value than many sparrows" (Matthew 10:29-31).

When we think of God's will, we may interpret it to be predestination. But it's the will of God for human beings to have freedom of choice. He allows us to exercise that freedom, even if we do it carelessly or in some other way we later regret. If He does not, we wouldn't be truly free. Nevertheless, even as we exercise our freedom, He knows us so intimately He has numbered every hair of our heads. And even though He is intimately concerned with what happens to one small sparrow, He is much more concerned with each event—no matter how insignificant it may seem—in our lives.

In coming chapters, we'll discuss the different perspectives on life found in the Books of Job, Proverbs, and Ecclesiastes. Although each book is divinely inspired, each looks at life from a different point of view. By developing the full-orbed view of life found in these three books, we can better respond to the events of our lives, even those that introduce pain and suffering. It may be we'll never be completely free of suffering in this life, but we can discover God's strength and comfort in the midst of our painful disappointments.

9
What Is Your View of Life?

When we confront suffering, we respond from the perspective of how we think life works. For many, this is a cause-and-effect view of life. The idea is, there is a cause for every effect and we want to find out what caused our suffering. What did we do wrong? Did someone else do something wrong? How can we avoid this sort of thing happening again?

But what if there's more than one valid perspective on life? Can different situations be viewed accurately with only one of these perspectives? The three wisdom books of Job, Proverbs, and Ecclesiastes present two views of life. Essentially, Job and Ecclesiastes agree in their perspective; Proverbs presents another point of view. The books seem to balance each other intentionally. This is especially interesting since both Proverbs and Ecclesiastes are strongly influenced by Solomon.

These three books present two types of wisdom literature. As its name implies, the Book of Proverbs consists of proverbial wisdom, short, pithy rules for personal happiness and welfare. These sayings generally condense experiential wisdom and offer acute observations about life.[95] Job and Ecclesiastes, on the other hand, are composed of contemplative or speculative wisdom that examines the basic problems of human existence, including the meaning of life and the problem of suffering.[96]

Proverbs

First let's consider the Book of Proverbs. The wisdom of Proverbs is intended primarily to provide an education in life to the young.[97] The specific audience was apparently Solomon's son,[98] for whom the book was prepared as part of his training to assume royal responsibilities. The phrase "my son" appears more than twenty times in the book.

The Book of Proverbs sees the world as generally predictable and equitable. But we must remember when we read the Bible to pay careful attention to the genre of the literature. In other words, although the Bible is inspired by God, it consists of a wide variety of kinds of literature, which must be read and interpreted according to the way literature works. The kinds of literature found in the Bible include, but they aren't limited to, a form of history, poetry, personal letters, apocalyptic prophecy, and proverbs. It's quite easy to see we don't interpret personal letters in the same way we interpret history, nor do we interpret proverbs as we would apocalyptic literature. To read one kind of literature like another is to misread and misinterpret the text. So how are we to interpret proverbs?

By definition, proverbs are generalizations, not hard-and-fast rules. Following them does not guarantee that specific results are always certain. If we interpret the proverbs as promises, we'll be disappointed. The proverbs tell us how things usually work, but they don't tell us how to control life or other people. For example, rather than spending money learning martial arts, I've depended heavily on Proverbs 15:1: "A soft answer turns away wrath." So far, it's worked very well! But I do realize I could give someone a soft answer and they could still punch me in the nose. The proverbs are not about how to manipulate other people. They don't overrule freedom of choice.

For example, many parents think Proverbs 22:6 is a guarantee that if children are raised properly, they will always do right. The proverb reads, "Train up a child in the way he should go, and when he is old he will not depart from it." Does this mean godly parents can train their children in such a way they will never depart from God, or if they do depart, they will return to God later in life? This statement has validity as a general principle, but it's not an absolute law. If parents could guarantee their children would live for God, it would compromise the biblical teaching concerning individual free will and moral responsibility. Children are not machines guaranteed to respond in certain ways if parents press the right buttons and pull the correct levers. They're human beings, and central to being human is the power of choice. Therefore, in interpreting this proverb, we should keep two things in mind: First, children are individuals created in the image of God. Each human being is unique, gifted with an unduplicated combination of talents and dreams. Severe problems can arise when parents try to live out their own dreams through their children, or when they try to compare one child with another.

Proverbs 22:6 addresses one of the greatest challenges parents face: helping each child reach his full personal potential. Parents should train up each child in the way he or she personally should go. Of course, parents should train every child to serve God, but more specifically, they should carefully assess each child's uniqueness and train him or her accordingly. They should encourage their children to develop their personal gifts. They should not expect their children to follow dutifully what to them is a dull profession, regardless of how long a line of ancestors practiced it. The child is a miracle of creation, fearfully and wonderfully made in the image of God. His or her gifts are far too precious to stifle in a musty mold made for someone else.

109

Second, children are sinners by birth. Sometimes they will fail. Parents can do nothing to guarantee their children will always make right choices. The only perfect father who ever lived had two children, a son and a daughter. He raised them both in a carefully designed environment free from negative peer pressure. They didn't have to struggle with the negative influences of pop culture. The father demonstrated his love for his children in a thousand ways. He spent quality time with them. Yet both children sinned rebelliously against their father. Some would have considered that a 100 percent failure rate.

The father was God. The children were Adam and Eve, and they originally did not have a sinful nature. If God had arranged things so Adam and Eve could not have failed, instead of human beings, they would have been puppets. But the love of a puppet is meaningless. Love is what it is only because it's a choice. All the promises of the gospel are to those who make conscious decisions to choose to serve the Lord.

No, Proverbs 22:6 is not a guarantee that parents can control the decisions their children will make in the future. Instead, the verse focuses on the individuality of the child and the duty of the parents to help their children become what God intended them to be.[99]

An interesting thing about proverbs is how they sometimes seem to conflict with one another. For example, one non-biblical proverb says, Absence makes the heart grow fonder. But another goes, Out of sight, out of mind. Which is it? I suppose it would depend on the circumstances and whether one really does love the person who is absent. But surely we would find no such tension in inspired proverbs, would we? Take a look at Proverbs 26:4-5. Verse 4 reads, "Do not answer a fool according to his folly, lest you also be like him." But the next verse reads, "Answer a fool according to his folly, lest he be

110

wise in his own eyes." Those who don't understand the nature of proverbs may think these are contradictions. They're not. There are two possible ways to answer a fool, depending on the desired outcome.

The advice Proverbs offers is to pursue a life of wisdom and righteousness. If you do, the result will tend to be positive, including long life, peace, divine blessing, happiness, health, and joy. Those who do not pursue a life of wisdom will tend to experience the negative consequences of early death, divine displeasure, disappointment, sickness, and grief. But there's no hard-and-fast guarantee things will work out precisely this way. The Bible records the stories of many wise and righteous people who died young—like Stephen, the first Christian martyr—suffered with sickness and disease that were never healed—like the prophet Elisha—or experienced grief and sadness in life, like the faithful sufferers of Hebrews 11. The King James Version indicates the general nature of the proverbs by actually supplying the word "tendeth" in several places.

The Book of Proverbs is a wonderful book of inspired, wise sayings. It's divided into thirty-one chapters, and it has often been recommended to read one chapter each day, matching the day of the month. In other words, on the first day of the month, read chapter 1, and so forth. If you do this for one year, you will have read through the Book of Proverbs twelve times during the course of the year, and you'll begin to think and make decisions based on the wisdom you're internalizing from this book. But remember, it's a book of proverbs. Don't lose faith in God if you attempt to follow one of the wise sayings and things don't work out as you hoped. You can control only what you do; you can't control the decisions and actions of others.

111

Job

In addition to Proverbs, Job is one of the three wisdom books of the Old Testament. This ancient book describes but doesn't explain the undeserved suffering of a righteous man. Many people know something about the story of Job; even people who have never read the book have some idea what is meant by the phrase, "the patience of Job." But those words actually appear in the New Testament. James wrote, "Behold, we count them happy which endure. Ye have heard of the patience of Job, and have seen the end of the Lord; that the Lord is very pitiful, and of tender mercy" (James 5:11, KJV). The way this is rendered in the New Living Translation is helpful: "We give great honor to those who endure under suffering. Job is an example of a man who endured patiently. From his experience we see how the Lord's plan finally ended in good, for he is full of tenderness and mercy."

Those who are convinced suffering has no place in the life of faith have attempted to find a way to blame Job for his suffering. But that idea is disallowed by the first verse of the Book of Job: "There was a man in the land of Uz, whose name was Job; and that man was blameless and upright, and one who feared God and shunned evil." We will look at the Book of Job in more detail in chapter 10, but for now we should note that regardless of what else we may read later in the book, we can't blame Job for the loss and suffering he experienced. He was blameless. He was upright. He feared God. He shunned evil. If there's always a cause-and-effect relationship between what we do and the level of peace and prosperity or suffering and poverty in our lives, Job could be expected to experience only prosperity and peace. There was no one like him on earth. We know this because God Himself said, "There is none like him on the earth, a blameless and upright man, one who fears God and shuns evil" (Job 1:8).

Not only are many people familiar with the phrase "the patience of Job," many have also heard of "Job's comforters." These three friends of Job believed in the theory of retribution. In other words, they believed Job's suffering was due to some specific sin he had committed. For thirty-five chapters, Job's friends wrongly insisted he had surely done something to deserve his suffering, and Job insisted he hadn't. His three original friends were joined by Elihu, whose argument was somewhat different but who was nevertheless off target. Finally, God interrupted these arguments with a question that revealed the error of all these attempts to find the cause for Job's suffering. God asked, "Who is this who darkens counsel by words without knowledge?" (Job 38:2). This is another way of saying Job's friends didn't know what they were talking about.

Nowhere in the book does God reveal to Job the cause of his suffering. Only the reader receives insight into the mysterious events in the throne room of Heaven. Satan entered God's presence and engaged in a conversation that had devastating consequences for Job. This innocent man didn't know God was the one who directed Satan's attention to him, but doubtless it wouldn't have helped Job if he had known. In any case, this fact further complicates any idea that a law of retribution was at work.

Job's friends were convinced Job's suffering was directly connected to some great unconfessed sin he had committed. Job agreed there should be a direct link between sin and suffering, but he complained that in his case this theory failed. He had done what was right, but he still suffered the loss he thought was reserved for the wicked. It seems significant that Satan has a high profile in the instigation of Job's sufferings but is absent from the events surrounding the end of the suffering and the reinstitution of blessing. If the law of retribution had been at work, it seems God would have permitted Satan to try him in response to some specific sin and that when Job had been sufficiently chastised Satan would have been recalled. But God offered no reason for singling Job out, other than to say he was a perfect man, and He offered no rationale for the conclusion of the suffering.

The wisdom arising from the Book of Job is that God is sovereign and has no obligation to explain Himself or His actions to humans. Even in the midst of unexplained and undeserved suffering, people are to honor God. Indeed, they find freedom only as they acknowledge God's freedom and as they refrain from demanding that God operate according to human rules.[100] The Book of Job utterly refutes the notion of a mechanistic, impersonal universe. It reveals the simple truth in the most dramatic of terms: people need God more than they need answers.

Ecclesiastes

The Book of Ecclesiastes is more a companion of Job than of Proverbs. While the initial impression may be that the book is the work of a thoroughgoing cynic who views all of life as meaningless, closer examination indicates that it—like Proverbs—targets a youthful audience, urging them to remember the Creator by keeping His commandments in view of the certainty of final judgment.[101]

The author of Ecclesiastes is a realist. He is concerned about the realities of life on planet earth. The phrase "under the sun" appears twenty-seven times in the book. The author is not really a cynic who has given up on life; he has discovered, through a lifetime of experimentation, that life cannot be reduced to a set of ironclad rules guaranteed to work every time. The reason for this is the curse placed upon the earth and human existence and relationships in Genesis 3. The phrase "under the sun" could be understood as a metaphor for "under

114

the curse." Because of the effect of sin, much about life is paradoxical. Life must be lived as it is; it's senseless to struggle against the curse in a vain attempt to escape it or outwit it. Even extreme righteousness will not enable a person to escape the negative effects of sin. The wise person will enjoy the good things in this world, and he will endure the not so good. The goal of the "Preacher" is a life of balance.

Like Job, Ecclesiastes teaches the freedom of God. Unlike Proverbs, the book describes the limits of human wisdom and ability. From the perspective of a person standing on planet earth—or "under the sun"—life is unpredictable and unfair. This is expressed in the words of Ecclesiastes 9:2: "All things come alike to all: one event happens to the righteous and the wicked; to the good, the clean, and the unclean; to him who sacrifices and him who does not sacrifice. As is the good, so is the sinner; he who takes an oath as he who fears an oath." If there is a system of retribution, the curse has damaged it beyond human ability to repair. The best advice, then, is to enjoy life as God gives it, with no resentment for seeming inequities. Within the parameters of godly living, life is to be enjoyed as a gift from God. There's no way to eliminate the consequences of the curse; it's best to work with them. Though the rewards for right living may be long in coming, and though the wicked may seem to prosper, ultimately it will go well for those who do right and evil for those who reject God's ways. The book expresses this in the following way.

> Because the sentence against an evil work is not executed speedily, therefore the heart of the sons of men is fully set in them to do evil. Though a sinner does evil a hundred times, and his days are prolonged, yet I surely know that it will be well with those who fear God, who fear before

Him. But it will not be well with the wicked; nor will he prolong his days, which are as a shadow, because he does not fear before God (Ecclesiastes 8:11-13).

In view of all that has gone before, the closing words of the book help us to gain eternity's perspective on earthly wisdom: "Fear God and keep His commandments, for this is man's all. For God will bring every work into judgment, including every secret thing, whether good or evil" (Ecclesaistes 12:13-14).

Summary

One could not gain a complete, balanced view of life from Proverbs alone, or from Job and Ecclesiastes together without the influence of Proverbs. As Proverbs suggests, there do seem to be general principles at work in life. Normally, with almost statistical probability, things go better for those who follow certain rules of right living. But the principles of Proverbs cannot take precedence over the person of God and His sovereign right to do all things after the counsel of His will, nor can they negate human freedom to make personal choices. Job and Ecclesiastes balance the "principle" approach to life with the equally true observation that specific results are not necessarily tied to prescribed behavior. Above and beyond all is the God who may, for His own purposes, do things differently from the way He usually does them.

All three wisdom books agree we are to live life in the fear of God. To fear God will generally produce pleasant results. But even if it does not, God is still to be feared and obeyed. His commands are more important than explanations; His sovereignty is more sacred than human demands for justice.[102]

Although we may better understand some episodes of suffering in our lives by contemplating the wisdom of Proverbs, it may be that in other circumstances our experiences will more closely parallel those found in Ecclesiastes or even in the Book of Job, one of the Bible's great heroes of faith, whose endurance in suffering—even when he had done nothing to deserve it—finds special mention in one of the earliest books of the New Testament.

10
Job: A Man Who Suffered without Knowing Why

A few days before I began writing this chapter I received an email advertising a new book on the problem of suffering. The book, written by a university professor, claims that the Bible does not answer this problem. According to the editorial review in Publisher's Weekly, the author thinks the answers given in the Bible about the problem of suffering are contradictory. In his view, the Old Testament prophets think that God sends pain and suffering as punishment for sin and that suffering is the result of the oppression of some people by others. On the other hand, he sees the stories of Joseph and Jesus as indicating that God uses suffering for redemptive purposes. Then again, the book's author sees the Book of Job as evidence that pain is God's test. Because he cannot accept these diverse perspectives on suffering he finds in Scripture, the professor gives up on his Christian faith and decides to respond to suffering and evil in two simple ways. First, he makes life as pleasing to himself as possible, then he makes it pleasing to others.

This regrettable response to the problem of suffering underscores the importance of coming to grips with this most troubling human problem from the perspective of faith in God. If our faith is not firmly rooted in the belief that there is a God and He is a good God who—as Abraham said—does what is right, we will lose our way in the midst of pain's inevitability. But when we trust God, we can survive life's disappointments to see a better day because we know that, regardless of the reason for our suffering, God loves us and He is on our side.

In chapter 9, we looked briefly at the Books of Job, Proverbs, and Ecclesiastes, and we noted their different perspectives on life. I mentioned that we would come back in this chapter and take another look at the Book of Job. This amazing story deserves careful consideration by those who wish to obtain a full perspective on the problem of suffering. Before we look at the book itself, notice that Job is mentioned in two other books of Scripture. First, he is mentioned twice in Ezekiel 14, along with Noah and Daniel. In an explanation of the reason for His judgment of Judah by allowing them to be in captivity in Babylon, God said, "Even if these three men, Noah, Daniel, and Job, were in it, they would deliver only themselves by their righteousness" (Ezekiel 14:14).[103] What this tells us about the spiritual condition of Judah is instructive, but for our purposes it is also important to see what this tells us about Job by comparing him with Noah and Daniel.

Noah is pictured in Genesis as the one man on the face of the earth who—in the midst of gross wickedness and rebellion against God—found grace in God's eyes. This is found in Genesis 6:5-9.

> Then the Lord saw that the wickedness of man was great in the earth, and that every intent of the thoughts of his heart was only evil continually. And the Lord was sorry that He had made man on the earth, and He was grieved in His heart. So the Lord said, "I will destroy man whom I have created from the face of the earth, both man and

beast, creeping thing and birds of the air, for I am sorry that I have made them." But Noah found grace in the eyes of the Lord. . . . Noah was a just man, perfect in his generations. Noah walked with God.

Notice the description of Noah as a just and perfect man, a man who walked with God. In spite of the overwhelming debauchery of his environment, Noah maintained his integrity with God. He refused to conform to the debased values of those around him.

The story of the second of these three men, Daniel, is well known. Of the three men mentioned by Ezekiel, Daniel is the only one who actually was in captivity in Babylon. He faced a variety of challenges to his faith. These included the opportunity to violate his convictions in order to honor the king's request and the challenge of those who schemed to have him thrown in the den of lions. But Daniel had purposed in his heart that he would not defile himself, and he also refused to compromise his prayer life to avoid the lions' den. As it relates to the comparison between Daniel and Job, it is important to note that when the king came to see whether Daniel had survived the night with the lions, Daniel said, "O king, live forever! My God sent His angel and shut the lions' mouths, so that they have not hurt me, because I was found innocent before Him; and also, O king, I have done no wrong before you" (Daniel 6:21-22). Noah was just and perfect; Daniel was innocent. So how does Job compare to them?

The second book of the Bible in which Job is mentioned other than in the book of Job is James, thought by some scholars to be the first book to be written in the New Testament. In the context of a discussion of the dangers of grumbling, James wrote,

My brethren, take the prophets, who spoke in the name of the Lord, as an example of suffering and patience. Indeed we count them blessed who endure. You have heard of the perseverance of Job and seen the end intended by the Lord—that the Lord is very compassionate and merciful (James 5:10-11).

This reference to Job in the New Testament is, like Ezekiel's reference to Job, quite useful in helping us grasp the biblical view of this man. James referred to the prophets as examples of suffering and patience, but when he wished to hold up a specific person as an example, that person was Job. Job is outstanding among of all of those who suffered in faith during the era of the Old Testament. His perseverance in the midst of his trial was without parallel. Further, his story reveals God is not vindictive and cruel; instead, He is compassionate and merciful. If we want to read a story about the blessings of endurance, that story is found in the Book of Job.

I wanted to take a look at how Job fared in the perspective of Ezekiel and James before we discuss the Book of Job, because it has become increasingly common for some to accuse Job of bringing his suffering on himself. We will see in the Book of Job that this idea is wrong, but we have already seen by the way Job is presented in other books that it's wrong to blame him for his suffering. Like Noah, Job was just and perfect. Like Daniel, he was innocent. For James, Job was a supreme example of patience in suffering. Now let's take a look at the Book of Job itself.

We need to remember when we read the Book of Job that this is one of the most ancient stories found in the Old Testament. Job was apparently a contemporary of Abraham, whose story begins to be told in the last verses of Genesis

11. We know this because there is no mention in the Book of Job of the law of Moses, Job's wealth was measured in cattle, and Job regularly offered burnt offerings. This was prohibited under the law of Moses. Since Abraham lived about four centuries before Moses received the law on Sinai, Job must have lived during this same era of time. One of the things this indicates that is significant for our reading of this book is that Job lived long before there was any written Scripture, since the writing of Scripture began with Moses. Therefore, Job faced this intense trial of his faith without being able to seek comfort or guidance from any written revelation. We must also remember Job did not have the Book of Job to read! He had no way of knowing why all of this was happening to him, and he had no way of knowing in advance how it was going to turn out. All Job had was his faith in God, a God he had come to know not on the basis of reading about Him in the Bible, but on the basis of what could be known about God by observing His creation, by listening to the voice of conscience, by any personal revelation God may have given him, and perhaps by what was communicated to him by his ancestors. All of this makes the first verse of the Book of Job all the more remarkable: "There was a man in the land of Uz, whose name was Job; and that man was blameless and upright, and one who feared God and shunned evil" (Job 1:1).

We must pay careful attention to how the book introduces Job. If we do, we will not fall prey to the idea that Job was to blame for his sufferings. As we are introduced to him, we discover Job was blameless and upright. He feared God and did not engage in evil. As we read the story, therefore, we must place no blame on Job. If we do, we miss the whole point of the story.

Lest we think this opinion of Job was merely the view of some human author of this book, we should note how Job is portrayed in the encounter between the Lord and Satan found in Job 1:6-8.

> Now there was a day when the sons of God came to present themselves before the Lord, and Satan also came among them. And the Lord said to Satan, "From where do you come?" So Satan answered the Lord and said, "From going to and fro on the earth, and from walking back and forth on it." Then the Lord said to Satan, "Have you considered My servant Job, that there is none like him on the earth, a blameless and upright man, one who fears God and shuns evil?"

Here we can see that God Himself evaluated Job as a blameless and upright man. Since God said Job was blameless, it indicates that the reader of the book is not to assign blame to Job for the events recorded in the book. Again, if we do, we will misconstrue the book's message, missing its point entirely.

After God asked Satan if he had considered the blameless and upright Job, Satan responded with these words:

> Does Job fear God for nothing? Have You not made a hedge around him, around his household, and around all that he has on every side? You have blessed the work of his hands, and his possessions have increased in the land. But now, stretch out Your hand and touch all that he has, and he will surely curse You to Your face! (Job 1:9-11).

These words tell us a great deal about how Satan thinks. He presumes that people serve God because of the material benefits they receive. He cannot fathom that people would serve God because they love Him and trust Him with their lives, not only on this earth but also for life after death. To Satan, if a person doesn't serve God for the material benefits, he serves God for nothing. Satan can't conceive there is something of far greater importance than material and temporal prosperity. In his view, everything is wrapped up with enjoying a life of pleasure and plenty on this earth. He was convinced that if God removed Job's material blessings, Job would curse God to His face.

The Lord responded to this challenge by saying to Satan, "Behold, all that he has is in your power; only do not lay a hand on his person" (Job 1:12). At this point in the story, we may begin to get nervous. The first question that pops into our minds is, "Why would God do such a thing?" We're great ones to question. We want to know why. And if we can't figure out why, we may be prone, like the author of the book I mentioned earlier, to abandon our faith in God.

At this point I must say if our faith in God depends on being able to understand and approve of every decision God makes, we are on a slippery slope to despair. If we look at this attitude carefully, we will note it is quite arrogant and presumptuous. We are not only assuming to be on God's level, but we are also sitting in judgment on God. Believing this means our god is very small and limited, a god much like us. We are collapsing the distinction between the Creator and the created. Many who have given up their faith because they cannot understand and approve of God's decisions have not actually given up faith in the true God at all; they have given up faith in a caricature of God shaped in their own image. They may have never actually had faith in the true God, who created all things for His own pleasure. (See Revelation 4:11.) Scripture nowhere indicates that God owes us an explanation for His decisions or that He does what He does for our approval. He is God. We would be well-advised to remember that with humility and reverence.

125

So far, we have seen in the Book of Job that Job was blameless. Since we're already familiar with how the story develops and ends, we know Job was not serving God for material benefits. He was serving God because he truly trusted Him. But Satan didn't know this. And as shocked and disappointed as we may be with the fact that God put Job in Satan's power, we should also notice that God placed a limitation on what Satan could do to Job. God said, "Behold, all that he has is in your power; only do not lay a hand on his person" (Job 1:12). This lets us know that ultimately, God is in control. Satan, we might say, is on a leash. He can go only as far as God permits.

Job's life was about to change radically. In one day, he received four devastating reports. First, he got the news that the Sabeans had stolen his five hundred yoke of oxen and his five hundred donkeys and killed the servants who had looked after the animals. While the servant who brought this report was still speaking, another arrived with more bad news. Fire had burned all of Job's sheep, consuming also the servants with them. Before the words were out of this servant's mouth, another arrived to report the Chaldeans had stolen Job's three thousand camels and killed Job's servants. But the worst news came last: Job's seven sons and three daughters had all died in the collapse of the house where they were gathered.

What would Job do? His loss was indescribable. He had gone in one day from being the wealthiest man in his part of the world, a man with a large, loving family, to being a childless pauper. Surely he would at least ask the question we consider so important, "Why?" Surely he would ask God to explain Himself! Would he wonder if it was, after all, worthwhile to serve God? We can imagine Satan standing on the sidelines, waiting eagerly for Job to fulfill his prediction. Satan was sure Job would curse God to His face.

But, no. Job's response to radical loss was breathtaking. He tore his robe and shaved his head, signs of mourning in the ancient world, and fell to the ground to worship God. In words that have become immortal, Job said, "Naked I came from my mother's womb, and naked shall I return there. The Lord gave, and the Lord has taken away; blessed be the name of the Lord" (Job 1:21). To us, this seems incredible. Rather than cursing God or even questioning God, Job worshiped God in the face of his loss. It is important to note he did not deny his suffering. He did not pretend nothing was wrong. He did not claim he was not hurting. He embraced his suffering by mourning, but his mourning was tempered by his trust in God. Job recognized that everything he had was a gift from God and it was God's prerogative to remove what He had given.

Job's response was so unexpected, so unlike what we think it would have been, that some have tried to fault Job even at the point of his suffering. Some say God only gives; He does not take away. Thus, Job was wrong in his assessment of the situation. Not only was Job wrong, he must have done something to deserve his suffering. At this point some turn to Job's words in Job 3:25 in order to pin the blame on the sufferer. Job said, "For the thing I greatly feared has come upon me, and what I dreaded has happened to me." Thus, according to some, Job's suffering was the result of his fear. If only he had not been afraid of losing his wealth and children, this would never have happened. In this view, fear is a kind of negative faith that attracts its object to itself. But this does not only misunderstand Job; it also misunderstands biblical faith. Faith is not a force that attracts its object; it is trust in God regardless of the circumstances of life.

These attempts to get the jump on Job's comforters by blaming him for his own problems even before his friends showed up must be rejected. The text of Scripture will not allow it. Immediately after Job confessed that the Lord gave and the Lord had taken away, the inspired text says, "In all this Job did not sin nor charge God with wrong" (Job 1:22). When Job said, "The Lord gave," he was right. And he was right when he said, "The Lord has taken away."

This was not what Satan expected. He thought for sure Job would have abandoned his faith in God. But Satan did not understand faith. He did not understand why people serve God. He was so frustrated by Job's response to his suffering he took advantage of another opportunity to further test his theory that there must come a point at which people will renounce their faith in God. We will explore that in the next chapter.

In the meantime, remember that Job is an example of the power of genuine faith. Even though he did not have the advantages we do—he had no Bible to read and he lived in the era before the coming of our Lord Jesus Christ and the pouring out of God's Holy Spirit—Job was able to retain his trust in God based on what we could call lesser revelation. But that is the power of faith. Faith cannot be conquered by pain and suffering. Faith endures even when there is no answer. Faith longs for God more than it insists on reasons.

11
Job's Situation Gets Even Worse

As we looked at the story of Job in chapter 10, we discovered we can't blame Job for the loss of his wealth and the death of his children. He had done nothing to deserve these tragic events, and he did not falsely accuse God when he said, "The Lord gave, and the Lord has taken away" (Job 1:21). Job, a blameless and upright man, had no idea his suffering originated in a conversation between the Lord and Satan. When Satan declared Job would curse God to His face if God removed His blessings, the Lord responded, "Behold, all that he has is in your power; only do not lay a hand on his person" (Job 1:12). In an attempt to prove his point, Satan engineered a series of events that resulted in the loss of Job's oxen, donkeys, sheep, camels, and the death of most of Job's servants. Then, in a final and devastating blow, Job's seven sons and three daughters all died in the collapse of the house where they had gathered.

But instead of cursing God, Job mourned and then worshiped God with these words: "Naked I came from my mother's womb, and naked shall I return there. The Lord gave, and the Lord has taken away. Blessed be the name of the Lord" (Job 1:21). Were it not for the next verse, we might think Job falsely accused God when he said, "The Lord has taken away."

But we would be mistaken, for Job 1:22 reads, "In all this Job did not sin nor charge God with wrong." It was, after all, God who had given Satan freedom to bring calamity upon Job. But the story does not end here.

For a second time, Satan appeared before the Lord. In an encounter very much like the one recorded in the first chapter of the book, the Lord said to Satan, "From where do you come?" Satan answered, "From going to and fro on the earth, and from walking back and forth on it" (Job 2:2). In words identical to those in the first encounter, the Lord asked, "Have you considered My servant Job, that there is none like him on the earth, a blameless and upright man, one who fears God and shuns evil?" Then, reflecting the failure of Satan's attempt to get Job to curse God, the Lord continued, "And still he holds fast to his integrity, although you incited Me against him, to destroy him without cause" (Job 2:3).

At this point, we should notice that Satan's accusation— Job would curse God if his blessings were removed—incited God to destroy His servant without cause. These words may trouble us. How could Satan incite God to do anything, much less destroy a person of faith without cause? Although it may help us understand what's going on here, the New Living Translation may not comfort us: "He has maintained his integrity, even though you persuaded me to harm him without cause." Why did God claim to be involved with Job's suffering? The reason for this is, Satan could not have touched Job unless God permitted it.

The story of Job is so strange to us, so foreign to our expectations, so much in conflict with our notions of the "good life" we think good people should enjoy, it's no surprise some people want to find a way to blunt its sharp edge. Surely all of this couldn't happen to an innocent man! Above all, surely

God could not be involved in this suffering. Something is wrong with this picture. But no, we understand it correctly. Job was blameless. Through no fault of his own—unless it is a fault to be so full of faith—he endured incredible suffering simply as a result of Satan's challenge to the Lord, a challenge the Lord accepted by giving Satan permission to do anything to Job but take his life.

Some people may say they could never serve a God who would do such a thing. Like the professor we talked about in chapter 10, they may give up on their faith because they cannot accept what Scripture says about suffering. It's up to you to make your choice. The problem we face is that we see no value in suffering. We tend to think all suffering is bad, and pleasure is good. Pain is evil, we think, so surely God would never inflict pain on anyone, nor would He allow Satan to do so. But we need to rethink this. In the long run, there could be many benefits to pain.

For example, the body's capacity for pain is beneficial in that it alerts us when something is wrong, when something is malfunctioning, when something needs attention. It would be dangerous and potentially deadly to be unable to sense physical pain. Likewise, C. S. Lewis, in his book The Problem of Pain, wrote that pain is God's megaphone. He said, "Pain insists upon being tended to. God whispers to us in our pleasures, speaks to us in our conscience, but shouts in our pain: it is His megaphone to rouse a deaf world."[104] If physical pain has the potential of being for our benefit, is it possible emotional pain may also have this potential?

After the Lord pointed out that Job had not given up his faith in spite of his loss, Satan answered, "Skin for skin! Yes, all that a man has he will give for his life. But stretch out Your hand now, and touch his bone and his flesh, and he will surely curse You to Your face!" (Job 2:4-5). Satan has learned nothing. He is still convinced a person will curse God if his pain is sufficiently intense. Perhaps some people will not do this in the face of loss of wealth and even as a result of the death of their children, but surely—Satan thinks—when the pain is intense enough, and when it is up close and personal, people will give up their faith in God. Every man must have his price.

The Lord answered Satan, "Behold, he is in your hand, but spare his life" (Job 2:6). Again, we should notice that Satan could do nothing without God's permission. In the first test, God allowed Satan to do whatever he would with the exception that he could not touch Job himself. Now, in the second test, Satan could touch Job, but he could not kill him. We can derive a certain measure of comfort from knowing that whatever Satan may do, he can do no more than God permits.

We may not understand why God would allow Satan to do anything, but faith does not depend on knowing everything God knows. Faith is not based on knowing all the reasons why; faith is based on trust in God and the knowledge that He is a good God who does all things well. Although we may throw Romans 8:28 around much too freely, especially when we quote it to people just beginning to process their loss, it is nevertheless true that "all things work together for good to those who love God, to those who are the called according to His purpose." If there were no possibility for painful experiences with no apparent point, this verse would be meaningless. However, we need this verse because of suffering, and the verse is found in the midst of Paul's discussion of suffering. For example, Paul wrote, "For I consider that the sufferings of this present time are not worthy to be compared with the glory which shall be revealed in us" (Romans 8:18). This is precisely the perspective we must have when we suffer and, in the midst of it, adopt Job's attitude. We must be convinced this life is not all there is. We must be persuaded that however intense our suffering may be in this life, it will fade in comparison with the glory that is to come.

These words may seem harsh when our pain is fresh. It is right that we mourn for our losses. Grief is a gift from God to help us process our pain. As strong as Job's faith was, he mourned even before he worshiped. This does not displease God. Any idea that God is unhappy with our tears and questions is wrong. He is the one who enables us to cry. He is the one who gives us the ability to think and to ask questions. Since He understands better than we do the full scope of the pain and suffering that was introduced into the world and into human experience by the rebellion in the Garden of Eden, God knows and honors our need to mourn. But He also hopes we will turn to Him in our suffering so He can comfort us. He hopes we will know this life is not all there is, that our faith in a brilliant glory to come will help us know that our present darkness will not prevail.

Although Job did not have Paul's words to read, he had the kind of faith Paul commended. When Satan attacked Job for the second time, striking him with painful boils from the sole of his foot to the crown of his head, Job's trust in God did not waver. Now Job had lost not only his wealth and his children, but also his health. Sitting in the midst of ashes, Job scraped his boils with a piece of broken pottery. At this moment, his only remaining family member, his wife, urged Job to do the very thing Satan was sure he would do. She said, "Do you still hold fast to your integrity? Curse God and die!" (Job 2:9). After such intense loss and suffering, would Job finally abandon his faith? Pressure from family members can be very hard to resist. With his frail health and overwhelming grief, would Job weaken?

133

No, he answered, "You speak as one of the foolish women speaks. Shall we indeed accept good from God, and shall we not accept adversity?" (Job 2:10).

Had Job gone too far now? Was he guilty of accusing God falsely when he suggested God is the source not only of good, but also of adversity? No, for the very next phrase reads, "In all this Job did not sin with his lips" (Job 2:10). When Job said God both gives and takes away, he was right. When he said we receive both good and adversity from God, he was right. For Job, even the greatest adversity—death—was no reason to abandon his faith in God. In the midst of his friends' false accusations, Job said, "Though He slay me, yet will I trust him" (Job 13:15). When a person has this kind of trust in God, what can Satan do to him?

This man of faith soundly defeated Satan's scheme. Satan was wrong. When a person has genuine faith in God, that person will not lose faith regardless of the circumstances of life. Interestingly, Satan never showed up again in the Book of Job. He tried his best to expose faith as being selfish, and he failed. He had spared nothing in his attempt to expose faith as fraud. Disease had so emaciated Job that when his three friends came to mourn with him and comfort him, they did not even recognize him. Weeping and crying, they tore their robes and sprinkled dust on their heads. For seven days and nights, they did not speak to Job because they saw how great his grief was.[105]

In a variety of ways, the next thirty-five chapters record the friends' attempts to convince Job he must have done something terribly wrong to deserve all that had happened to him. Job agreed that he also would have thought these kinds of things happened as a direct result of sin, but he couldn't figure out what he had done. Job's response further reinforces the notion that he had no idea why these things had happened to him. He was not forewarned. God did not reveal to him that these kinds of tragedies were the result of some kind of cosmic conflict that would, in the end, turn out in his favor. Job was mystified. He knew he was in pain, but he didn't know why.

After Job's three friends gave up their efforts to convince Job of his sin, another person arrived on the scene. Elihu, a younger man, was angry with Job and his three friends. He had refrained from speaking previously because of his youth. But in his disappointment with the inability of Job's three friends to convince him of his sin, Elihu said, "Great men are not always wise, nor do the aged always understand justice" (Job 32:9). The urge to express his opinion was so strong he could no longer hold in his words. Elihu said, "Therefore listen to me, you men of understanding: far be it from God to do wickedness, and from the Almighty to commit iniquity. For He repays man according to his work, and makes man to find a reward according to his way. Surely God will never do wickedly, nor will the Almighty pervert justice" (Job 34:10-12).

Here is an example of a half-truth. Of course God will not sin; but Elihu did not realize Job's suffering was not an either-or matter. It was not a result of anybody's sin. Elihu thought if it was not due to Job's sin, then it had to be due to God's sin. And since that couldn't be, only one possibility remained: Job had sinned. Elihu thought very much like many who try to figure out why bad things happen to good people. They assume, like Elihu, that whatever happens to people is God's repayment for what they have done. The first thought in the minds of many is, I must have done something to cause this. God must be getting even with me. But like Job's other friends, Elihu was wrong.

We know that all of the attempts to pin blame on Job were wrong because when all the dust settled, the Lord answered Job out of a whirlwind: "Who is this who darkens counsel by words without knowledge? Now prepare yourself like a man; I will question you, and you shall answer me" (Job 38:1-3). With one question, God exposed the error of all that had previously been said about Job's situation. Job's friends did not know what they were talking about. They were wrong when they tried to pin the blame on Job.

After an extended speech about His creative acts, a speech that revealed the emptiness of human attempts to discover cause-and-effect relationships between the divine and human realms, God said to Job, "Shall the one who contends with the Almighty correct Him? He who rebukes God, let him answer it" (Job 40:2). The point is clear. Although we may have questions, it is fruitless to try to correct the Almighty. Some may think God is wrong. They may even abandon their faith in Him in the face of their suffering. But the problem is that since we are not God, we are not qualified to correct Him. We don't know what He knows. We can't see from His perspective. Our perspective is so limited, so earthbound. It would even be overstating the case to compare our attempts to correct God with the attempt of an ant to correct us. At least an ant has something in common with us; it is part of the created realm. But the gulf between the Creator and creation is so vast it is beyond comprehension. Although we are created in the image of God, we are not God.

Job's response to God's correction reveals his grasp of the vanity of trying to correct God. Job said, "Behold, I am vile. What shall I answer You? I lay my hand over my mouth. Once I have spoken, but I will not answer; yes, twice, but I will proceed no further" (Job 40:4-5). But the Lord was not finished with his questions for Job. He said, "Now prepare yourself like a man; I will question you, and you shall answer Me: Would you indeed annul My judgment? Would you condemn Me that you may be justified? Have you an arm like God? Or can you thunder with a voice like His?" (Job 40:6-9).

God offered further challenges that revealed Job's limitations. Then Job responded, "I know that You can do everything, and that no purpose of Yours can be withheld from You. You asked, 'Who is this who hides counsel without knowledge?' Therefore I have uttered what I did not understand, things too wonderful for me, which I did not know. Listen, please, and let me speak; You said, 'I will question you, and you shall answer Me.' I have heard of You by the hearing of the ear, but now my eye sees You. Therefore I abhor myself, and repent in dust and ashes" (Job 42:2-6).

From the beginning of the story, Job's faith had been intact. This shows us it is possible to have faith and questions simultaneously. His questions did not indicate a lack of faith. He asked them from the perspective of faith. When Job realized he could not understand, when he saw his questions were off target, he repented. He would ask no further. He would simply trust God.

At this point, the Lord said to one of Job's three friends, "My wrath is aroused against you and your two friends, for you have not spoken of Me what is right, as My servant Job has. Now therefore, take for yourselves seven bulls and seven rams, go to my servant Job and offer up for yourselves a burnt offering; and My servant Job shall pray for you. For I will accept him, lest I deal with you according to your folly; because you have not spoken of Me what is right, as My servant Job has" (Job 42:7-8). When Job prayed for his friends, the Lord restored Job's losses, giving him twice as much wealth as he had before the beginning of his suffering. Job's latter days were blessed more than the beginning. Now he possessed fourteen thousand sheep, six thousand camels, one thousand yoke of oxen, and one thousand donkeys. But best of all, he also had seven sons and three daughters.

Job, whose life had hung on a thread, lived to be 140 years old, enjoying his children and grandchildren to the fourth generation.

Satan's challenges and accusations were proven wrong. Genuine faith triumphs over pain and suffering. Job had many opportunities to turn his back on God: when he received the first report about the loss of his oxen and donkeys, when his children died in a windstorm, when his wife urged him to curse God and die, and when his friends hurled judgmental barbs at him. But Job accepted in faith what he could not understand. He didn't pretend he didn't hurt. He didn't retreat to an imaginary world of positive confessions. He acknowledged his pain and mourned his losses.

Job's tenacious faith had its reward. Think what he would have lost had he given up! Instead, he earned honorable mention in the New Testament: "Indeed we count them blessed who endure. You have heard of the perseverance of Job and seen the end intended by the Lord—that the Lord is very compassionate and merciful" (James 5:11).

You probably don't understand your suffering and pain. Few do. But regardless of what is happening in your life right now, and no matter how long it endures, you can be sure God intends—at the right time and place—to demonstrate to you His compassion and mercy. As difficult as it is, trust God and be patient. Don't cast away your confidence in God. There is certainly no answer there. The writer of the Book of Hebrews declared his readers had "joyfully accepted the plundering of [their] goods, knowing that [they had] a better and an enduring possession for [themselves] in heaven." He wrote, "Therefore do not cast away your confidence, which has great reward. For you have need of endurance, so that after you have done the will of God, you may receive the promise" (Hebrews 10:34-36).

12
Suffering as the Way to Strength

In II Corinthians 12, Paul told the story of a man who was caught up to the third heaven. He wasn't sure whether this was a visionary experience or whether the man was actually dead. As the story progresses, we discover the man was Paul himself.

In the verses immediately before this story, Paul compiled a list of the things he suffered during his ministry for Christ.

. . . In stripes above measure, in prisons more frequently, in deaths often. From the Jews five times I received forty stripes minus one. Three times I was beaten with rods; once I was stoned; three times I was shipwrecked; a night and a day I have been in the deep; in journeys often, in perils of waters, in perils of robbers, in perils of my own countrymen, in perils of the Gentiles, in perils in the city, in perils in the wilderness, in perils in the sea, in perils among false brethren; in weariness and toil, in sleeplessness often, in hunger and thirst, in fastings often, in cold and nakedness—besides the other things, what comes upon me daily: my deep concern for all the churches. Who is weak, and I am not weak? Who is made to stumble, and I do not burn with indignation?

If I must boast, I will boast in the things which concern my infirmity. The God and Father of our Lord Jesus Christ, who is blessed forever, knows that I am not lying. In Damascus the governor, under Aretus the king, was guarding the city of the Damascenes with a garrison, desiring to arrest me; but I was let down in a basket through a window in the wall, and escaped from his hands (II Corinthians 11:23-33).

This list of life-threatening experiences precedes his story about the man who was caught up to the third heaven. Before we look further at the story about Paul's heavenly revelations, think about what he has just said. How does Paul's description of his experiences as a Christian compare with the expectations many people today have of the Christian life? It is not uncommon now for people to think that becoming a Christian will end their problems or at least greatly minimize them. Christianity is often promoted as the way to the good life, even the way to material prosperity and abundant physical health. Verses scattered here and there throughout Scripture are isolated from their immediate and larger contexts and read to mean that if we are Christians, we can have whatever we want, we can possess whatever we confess, or we can manipulate the circumstances of life in our own favor. These claims would have shocked first-century Christians, who understood that to believe on Jesus was to put one's very life on the line. They knew what it meant to be ridiculed, persecuted, and rejected even by their families. Many of them knew what it meant for their life to hang by a thread. They knew what it meant to be in need, even of food and clothing. Would they recognize today's Christianity? Would they feel comfortable in today's churches?

In one of the earliest letters to be written in the New Testament, James said, "If a brother or sister is naked and destitute of daily food, and one of you says to them, 'Depart in peace, be warmed and filled,' but you do not give them the things which are needed for the body, what does it profit?" (James 2:15-16). Today, some have the notion that if a person is truly a believer, he will never experience destitution. In this view, someone claiming to be a believer who experiences lack of food and clothing should be rebuked for a lack of faith. Some claim it wouldn't help to give them what they need; they will just slip back into poverty again. But James turned this idea on its head. In the scenario he described, those who lack food and clothing are brothers and sisters in the Lord. And to help them in their time of need by giving them what they lack is a sign of genuine faith—faith that results in good deeds.

For Paul, suffering characterized genuine ministers of Christ; in contrast, it was false apostles who were self-centered, egotistical, intent on feathering their own nests, and who abused those they pretended to lead. Paul wrote, "For you put up with it if one brings you into bondage, if one devours you, if one takes from you, if one exalts himself, if one strikes you on the face" (II Corinthians 11:20). This was far from Paul's attitude toward the responsibility of Christian leaders. That's why he described his painful experiences in detail; they were experiences that could be expected by those who surrendered their lives to Christ. They were precisely the opposite of the experiences of those who were merely pretenders.

When we read the Scriptures in only one translation, we sometimes get so used to the words that we miss their force. So let's hear Paul's description of his experiences once more, this time from the New Living Translation.

> I know I sound like a madman, but I have served him far more! I have worked harder, been put in jail more often, been whipped times without number, and faced death again

141

and again. Five different times the Jews gave me thirty-nine lashes. Three times I was beaten with rods. Once I was stoned. Three times I was shipwrecked. Once I spent a whole night and a day adrift at sea. I have traveled many weary miles. I have faced danger from flooded rivers and from robbers. I have faced danger from my own people, the Jews, as well as from the Gentiles. I have faced danger in the cities, in the deserts, and on the stormy seas. And I have faced danger from men who claim to be Christians but are not. I have lived with weariness and pain and sleepless nights. Often I have been hungry and thirsty and have gone without food. Often I have shivered with cold, without enough clothing to keep me warm. Then, besides all this, I have the daily burden of how the churches are getting along. Who is weak without my feeling that weakness? Who is led astray, and I do not burn with anger? If I must boast, I would rather boast about the things that show how weak I am. God, the Father of our Lord Jesus, who is to be praised forever, knows I tell the truth. When I was in Damascus, the governor under King Aretas kept guards at the city gates to catch me. But I was lowered in a basket through a window in the city wall, and that's how I got away!

There were no limousines waiting to carry Paul from Damascus in comfort and honor. He had to sneak out of town. He endured not only excruciating physical pain again and again, but also emotional trauma, including struggles with anger. This is what led him to talk about his visit to the third heaven.

When Paul was caught up into Paradise, he "heard inexpressible words, which it is not lawful for a man to utter" (II Corinthians 12:4). After all he had suffered on earth, Paul was apparently tempted to boast about the great revelation he received while in Paradise. Instead, he continued by explaining his visit to Paradise was not an occasion for boasting, but for additional suffering.

> And lest I should be exalted above measure by the abundance of the revelations, a thorn in the flesh was given to me, a messenger of Satan to buffet me, lest I be exalted above measure. Concerning this thing I pleaded with the Lord three times that it might depart from me. And He said to me, "My grace is sufficient for you, for My strength is made perfect in weakness." Therefore most gladly I will rather boast in my infirmities, that the power of Christ may rest upon me. Therefore I take pleasure in infirmities, in reproaches, in needs, in persecutions, in distresses, for Christ's sake. For when I am weak, then I am strong (II Corinthians 12:7-10).

Like the story of Job, these words of Paul are so unlike what some people think the Christian life should be that they attempt to overthrow the force of his words by placing the blame on him for his suffering. It has even been suggested that Paul's problem was a lack of faith. If only he had had enough faith, he would have been able to get rid of his thorn in the flesh. As we will see, the inspired text of Scripture will not allow this interpretation.

Many Bible readers like to speculate about the nature of Paul's thorn in the flesh. For our present purposes, it is not important to know precisely what this thorn was. Whatever it was involved suffering. And whatever it was, it was given to Paul to prevent him from being exalted above measure because of the abundance of revelations he had received. Some surprising things are going on here. Let's look at Paul's words carefully.

143

First, revelation can be an occasion for pride. Paul's revelation involved insight into what was going on in Paradise. How tempting it would be to boast of one's spirituality after a visit to Paradise! How tempting it would be to write a book about this with full-color illustrations. How tempting it would be to go on the speaking circuit to tell everyone about it. But Paul knew he could not do this. If he were going to boast, it would be in his weaknesses, not in his revelations, not in his strengths.

Second, Paul's thorn in the flesh was given to him specifically to prevent him from getting "puffed up," as the New Living Translation puts it. Although we will soon discover an amazing parallel between the stories of Paul and Job, at this point there is a vital difference. As far as we know, Job was in no danger of being puffed up. His suffering was due to something else altogether. But there can be many reasons for suffering. Pain is not simplistic. It cannot be traced to one single cause. We can see from Paul's experience that humility is more important than freedom from pain. In other words, pride and arrogance are so spiritually devastating that God may allow us to suffer in order to prevent us from falling into their clutches.

Third—and here is where we see the parallel with Job— Paul's thorn in the flesh was "a messenger of Satan to buffet [him], lest [he] be exalted above measure" (II Corinthians 12:7). In even plainer language, Paul's thorn in the flesh was a messenger from Satan to torment him and keep him from getting proud (New Living Translation). Immediately we are compelled to ask, "How can Satan be an instrument for good in a believer's life?" This is so counterintuitive, so radical, that at first we may not want to believe it. But there it is in the inspired text. Paul didn't like it either, so he pleaded with the Lord three times that it would depart from him. Here is where some people fault Paul for his alleged lack of faith. If you think faith means our prayers will always be answered in the way we want them to be, you may wonder why Paul prayed unsuccessfully three times. But we soon learn the reason why his prayer was not answered had nothing to do with lack of faith.

Fourth, in response to Paul's prayers, God said, "My grace is sufficient for you, for My strength is made perfect in weakness" (II Corinthians 12:9). Rather than removing Paul's thorn in the flesh—the messenger of Satan—God explained to Paul that it is precisely in our weakness that God's strength is perfected. Again, this seems counterintuitive to us. We're supposed to be strong. We're supposed to have it all together. But the problem with this kind of thinking is that it focuses on us, not on Christ. It breeds self-sufficiency, self-centeredness, even arrogance—although these problems may be disguised as spiritual maturity or victorious Christian living.

Fifth, after God's surprising answer to his prayers reoriented Paul, he no longer wished for the removal of his thorn in the flesh. He no longer yearned for a pain-free life immune to suffering. He valued the genuine power of Christ so highly, and he understood the impossibility of compatibility between Christ's power and human exaltation so clearly, that he concluded the matter with the following words.

> Therefore most gladly I will rather boast in my infirmities, that the power of Christ may rest upon me. Therefore I take pleasure in infirmities, in reproaches, in needs, in persecutions, in distresses, for Christ's sake. For when I am weak, then I am strong (II Corinthians 12:9-10).

The idea presented here is not that we should be willing to embrace weakness if it is absolutely necessary. The idea is that weakness is the only way to strength. The greater our weakness,

145

the greater the opportunity for the power of Christ to rest upon us. The more fully we recognize our inabilities, the more we experience of Christ's abilities. It is not just a matter of tolerating weakness. Paul went from praying for deliverance from suffering to gratitude for suffering. "Most gladly," he said, "I will rather boast in my infirmities." He now took pleasure in infirmities, a word used in the Bible for weakness of any sort as well as for sickness. He took pleasure in reproaches, which means he was pleased when insulted or mistreated. He took pleasure in needs, which means he was pleased when he encountered distress and trouble. He was pleased when he was persecuted for his faith in Christ. He took pleasure in distresses, or in difficulty, trouble, and calamity.

How could Paul make such a radical about-face? How could he return from his visionary experience of Paradise and, in the face of incredible suffering, say he was pleased with so much pain? Here is his reason: "For when I am weak, then I am strong" (II Corinthians 12:10). Weakness is the way to strength. The abandonment of self-absorption is essential to a life of spiritual strength. We must not seek our own way. We must not seek to develop personal power. We must not seek freedom from suffering. Instead, we must seek the power of Christ.

Paul's story is troubling on a number of levels, not least of which is the role of suffering in spiritual development. Connected with this is the use of Satan as a positive instrument in producing humility in one's life. It is beyond our ability to explore this strange idea fully now, but we should note the following ideas: (1) In the cases of both Job and Paul, Satan was involved, but God limited that involvement. Satan was on a leash. Certainly Satan would have killed Job if he could have, and no doubt he would like to have terminated Paul. But he could not. God was in control. (2) God's priorities are not necessarily the same as our priorities. Job would never have chosen to experience such devastating loss. There was nothing attractive about the pain he endured. But Job could not see into the eternal realm. He could not know why God allowed Satan to do the things he did. He could not see the good that would ultimately come from his suffering. Even today, knowing the end of the story, we still wrestle with the idea that God gave Satan freedom to hurt Job the way he did. Like Job, Paul could not—at first—see any possible good coming from his suffering. He wanted to get rid of it. But when he understood the consequences of pride and the blessing of humility, Paul embraced his suffering with gladness, knowing it was the only way for him to develop spiritual strength.

Not by any means are all of the biblical accounts of suffering in the category of Job and Paul. Satan is not involved in every episode of suffering in the Bible. Not everyone who suffers does so because of an encounter between Satan and God, nor does everyone suffer because of the danger of pride and arrogance. But any thorough examination of the biblical teaching on suffering must include an examination of the stories of Job and Paul. It is still possible, after all, that some of those who suffer in faith today do fit into this category. The Bible stories are not given to us just to provide a historical account of those who have suffered in the past. They are there to provide examples to us, to teach us what it means to live a life of faith. And in the cases of Job and Paul, we learn that faith sometimes means not understanding. It sometimes means worshiping in the face of sorrow, pain, and suffering. It sometimes means unanswered questions.

From Paul's story we learn this powerful lesson: God's grace is all we need. In our weakness, His strength is perfected. When we are willing to embrace this truth—gladly facing all of the challenges that come along with it—spiritual strength is on the way. We too can be strong, even when we are weak.

13
Suffering for a Little While

In their book By Their Blood: Christian Martyrs of the Twentieth Century, James and Marti Hefley report that more people were martyred for their faith during the twentieth century than during the previous nineteen hundred years.[106] David Barnett, editor of World Christian Encyclopedia, estimates that as many as 160,000 people are killed each year for their faith in Christ.[107]

These regrettable facts underscore the reality of suffering for people of faith. Those who say that if Christians have enough faith they should be able to avoid suffering are simply wrong. They are like the proverbial ostrich with its head well-buried in the sand, oblivious to what is going on around them. Not only are they ignoring reality, they are misinformed as to what Scripture says about the very real possibility of suffering for those who name Christ as their Savior. According to the Bible, there can be many reasons for suffering. One of these reasons is the enmity against Christ that is often manifested by enmity against those who follow Christ.

Jesus said, "If the world hates you, you know that it hated Me before it hated you. If you were of the world, the world would love its own. Yet because you are not of the world, but I chose you out of the world, therefore the world hates you. Remember the word that I said to you, 'A servant is not greater than his master.' If they persecuted Me, they will also persecute you. If they kept My word, they will keep yours also. But all these things they will do to you for My name's sake, because they do not know Him who sent Me" (John 15:18-21). Jesus' point is clear. If we are identified with Him, people will respond to us the way they respond to Him.

In the Sermon on the Mount, Jesus said, "Blessed are those who are persecuted for righteousness sake, for theirs is the kingdom of heaven. Blessed are you when they revile and persecute you, and say all kinds of evil against you falsely for My sake. Rejoice and be exceeding glad, for great is your reward in heaven, for so they persecuted the prophets who were before you" (Matthew 5:10-12).

These words not only inform us that Christians can expect persecution, but they should respond with gladness and rejoicing. This may at first seem incredible. Why should we respond to suffering with gladness? Then we discover that to suffer for our faith identifies us not only with Jesus but also with all of those who have gone before us who have faced the hostility of an unbelieving world. The point is this: If we are suffering for our faith in Christ, we are doing something right. If our faith is so anemic that Christ's enemies take no note of it, we should be alarmed. But if we suffer persecution by those who reject Christ, it indicates that our faith is genuine and robust. This puts us in the company of all people of faith, from Abel to the first-century Christians and down to the present day.

The apostle John saw this connection with history. He wrote, "In this the children of God and the children of the devil are manifest: Whoever does not practice righteousness is not of God, nor is he who does not love his brother. For this is the

150

message that you heard from the beginning, that we should love one another, not as Cain who was of the wicked one and murdered his brother. And why did he murder him? Because his works were evil and his brother's righteous. Do not marvel, my brethren, if the world hates you" (I John 3:10-13).

It is regrettable that this enmity within families, which began with the first human family, is a continuing reality when some people in the family believe on Christ and others do not. Jesus addressed this problem: "Do not think that I came to bring peace on earth. I did not come to bring peace but a sword. For I have come to 'set a man against his father, a daughter against her mother, and a daughter-in-law against her mother-in-law'; and 'a man's enemies will be those of his own household'" (Matthew 10:34-36).

This problem is not unique to those of us living in the time after the advent of Christ. When Jesus said these words, He drew from the writings of the prophet Micah. Micah warned, "Do not trust in a friend; do not put your confidence in a companion; guard the doors of your mouth from her who lies in your bosom. For son dishonors father, daughter rises against her mother, daughter-in-law against her mother-in-law; a man's enemies are the men of his own household" (Micah 7:5-6).

The kinds of biblical verses we have been reading are not pleasant. We would rather not think about the possibility of suffering from any source, much less from our own family members that we love so much. And why is it that anyone would hate us for being Christians? Shouldn't everyone love us since we are more interested in their welfare and in what is good for the world, than we ever were before we came to know Christ?

But when we think this way we are forgetting there is a cosmic struggle between good and evil. We know the end of this struggle is already determined; Satan will be cast into the

151

lake of fire.[108] In the meantime, Satan continues to resist God's authority, fighting against God's purposes wherever he can, enlisting in his service as many of those who reject Christ as possible. Those who believe in Christ have victory over Satan. They can cast out demons.[109] They can cause Satan to flee from them by resisting him.[110] Still, this authority is in the spiritual realm. In the physical world, believers live side by side, perhaps even in the same house, with unbelievers. Even Jesus lived with unbelieving siblings who mocked His mission.[111] His family members thought He was out of his mind.[112] Others claimed Jesus was possessed by the ruler of demons.[113]

Most of us would like to have the approval of those around us. We don't want to be rejected. We don't want to be misunderstood. We gravitate toward those who understand us, who see things as we do. But we must make a decision. If we refuse to believe on Christ, that will please those who have also rejected Him. If we put our faith in Christ, we risk the disapproval of those who continue to reject Him. Which will it be?

When Peter wrote his first letter, his central theme was the appropriate Christian response to suffering. This suffering was the result of "various trials," including the abuse of servants by their masters and defamation by unbelievers. Peter saw this suffering as normal for believers. Christians share in Christ's sufferings simply because of their identification with Him. This suffering is nothing less than the will of God. To suffer patiently is commendable before God. Our Lord's suffering set the example for us, and we as Christians are called to submit to unjust suffering. If faithfully endured, the result of this suffering will be "praise, honor, and glory at the revelation of Jesus Christ." Those who keep their faith in Christ will survive the suffering perfected, established, strengthened, and settled.

The increasing secularization of Western culture and the increasing intolerance of Christianity by non-Christian religions in the world today have created an environment for Christians in the twenty-first century much like that of the last half of the first century. We can draw instruction, comfort, and hope from Peter's letter to suffering believers. If our spiritual ancestors could endure suffering victoriously, so can we. The same God they served will strengthen us. Let's read Peter's first letter as if it were written to us. Since it is part of God's Word to all who believe, it is indeed our letter.

The first notice we see of the possibility of suffering is found in I Peter 1:6-7. Peter wrote, "In this you greatly rejoice, though now for a little while, if need be, you have been grieved by various trials, that the genuineness of your faith, being much more precious than gold that perishes, though it is tested by fire, may be found to praise, honor, and glory at the revelation of Jesus Christ." It is always important to read Scripture in its context. When Peter wrote, "In this you greatly rejoice," he referred back to the final words in the previous verse concerning the "salvation ready to be revealed in the last time" (I Peter 1:5). We are looking ahead to the final outworking of our salvation. This world is not all there is. The pain we experience now is not permanent. As we confront the "various trials" that come our way, our grief is tempered by joy when we think about the temporary nature of these trials. As Peter said, they are "for a little while."

Both Peter and James wrote of our "various trials," using the same Greek words to describe them. James wrote, "My brethren, count it all joy when you fall into various trials, knowing that the testing of your faith produces patience" (James 1:2-3). Both Peter and James saw trials as cause for rejoicing. James recommended rejoicing because of the positive benefits

153

that testing develops in one's character.[114] Peter recommended rejoicing for the same reason, but also in view of the ultimate salvation that will result from the faith that trials prove to be genuine.

The "various trials" are apparently persecutions as opposed to the ordinary trials of life. We can expect ordinary trials to endure throughout our lifetime; they are the result of living in an imperfect world among imperfect people. But the trials in view here are immediate and brief; they are "for a little while."

Persecution for the sake of Christ proves the genuineness of one's faith. Those who have a mere profession of faith in Christ will not endure persecution; those who truly trust Him will continue to trust Him regardless of life's circumstances. The persecution that tries the believer's faith is like the fire that purifies gold by purging out the impurities. Even though purified gold lasts a very long time, it will eventually perish. As Peter pointed out, genuine faith is more valuable than gold; it will never perish.

The imagery of the righteous being tested by fire like precious metals is also found in the Hebrew Scriptures. Job, that great hero of faith, said, "He knows the way that I take; when He has tested me, I shall come forth as gold" (Job 23:10). Solomon wrote, "The refining pot is for silver and the furnace for gold, but the Lord tests the hearts" (Proverbs 17:3). Trials tend to purify motives.

According to Peter, faith that endures persecution will be "found to praise, honor, and glory at the revelation of Jesus Christ." Those whose faith has proven genuine will bring praise, honor, and glory to the Lord Jesus when He is revealed. They will also partake in some way in the glory that will accompany Christ's revelation. This will be due, at least in part, to the glorification of the believer's human body, which will be transformed so as to be like "his glorious body" (Philippians 3:21; I John 3:2).

When we compare the pain of suffering with the reward that awaits us for holding fast to our faith in the midst of suffering, our present pain no longer seems so overwhelming. Our hope puts our pain in its proper perspective.

In one of his most extensive treatments of suffering, Peter called on servants to be submissive to their masters, holding up the suffering of Christ as an example. He wrote,

> Servants, be submissive to your masters with all fear, not only to the good and gentle, but also to the harsh. For this is commendable, if because of conscience toward God one endures grief, suffering wrongfully. For what credit is it if, when you are beaten for your faults, you take it patiently? But when you do good and suffer, if you take it patiently, this is commendable before God. For to this you were called, because Christ also suffered for us, leaving us an example, that you should follow His steps: "Who committed no sin, nor was deceit found in His mouth"; who, when He was reviled, did not revile in return; when He suffered, He did not threaten, but committed Himself to Him who judges righteously (I Peter 2:18-23).

In view of the obvious repulsiveness of slavery to cultures that have been influenced by the Christian ethic of the equal value of all people, it at first seems strange that New Testament writers urged believing slaves to submit to their masters. By Roman law, "the head of a household could legally execute his slaves, and they would all be executed if the head of the household was murdered."[115] Although Roman law did recognize slaves as persons, it also declared them to be property. As property, they were

155

abused by some owners and treated as socially inferior by nearly all owners.[116] During the expansion of the Roman Empire, many of the conquered people were taken as slaves; some people had simply been kidnapped and forced into slavery. By the time of the first century, many slaves were the descendants of such victims. These first-century slaves were born in the household of their master.

There were three basic categories of slaves during the first century. The first, which Peter had in view when he wrote the passage we just read, consisted of household slaves. A second category was the field slaves, who did much of the agricultural work. A third category consisted of slaves who worked in the mines; they were abused most harshly and often died after only brief service in the mines.[117]

Slaves could be found in all professions. They were paid for their work and could entertain the possibility of eventually being able to purchase their freedom.[118] In many ways, household slaves found themselves in a situation superior to free peasants, most of whom worked "as tenant farmers on the vast estates of wealthy landowners."[119]

It would have been pointless for New Testament writers to lash out against the institution of slavery. They did not address their letters to political movers and shakers who perhaps could, if they would, do something about the problem. They wrote to believers who found themselves living in the full range of social relationships of the first century, including slavery. These believers needed to know how to live out their Christian faith where they were. We must be clear; slavery is diametrically opposed to the Christian ethic. But the harsh reality is that many first-century Christians were slaves. Like all who believed on Jesus, they needed to know what their faith in Christ meant for their practical day-to-day existence. This was the issue Peter addressed.

The servants to whom Peter wrote were household servants. Let's look closely at this text. The word translated "be submissive" has to do with deference and respect. Although it implies obedience, it is not unquestioning, unqualified obedience. It is voluntary submission.

One might think the command for servants to submit to their masters "with all fear" means that the servants are to fear their masters. But the context in which these words are found indicates this is the fear of God, as seen in the previous verse, I Peter 2:17. In that verse, it is God alone who is to be feared. Believers are not to fear human beings, as Peter pointed out in I Peter 3:14.

Servants are to "be submissive" to their masters, whether they are good and gentle or harsh. Peter had unbelieving masters in view here. Even the good and gentle masters were apparently unbelievers. If they had been believers, Peter would no doubt have written to them to inform them of their Christian duties, as did Paul.

Several of the New Testament letters include passages dealing with what we might call "house codes." The text we are discussing in I Peter is one such passage. These house codes addressed the relationships of members of a household, including husbands, wives, children, and servants. It is unfortunate that these texts have been used by some to justify slavery. Contrary to this notion, Paul encouraged those who came to the Lord while they were slaves to obtain their freedom, if possible. Even if it was impossible, believing slaves were not to view themselves as the slaves of people, but of Christ.[120] Paul told Philemon he should no longer treat Onesimus as a slave but as a brother. The New Testament's message of equality and

157

freedom is so powerful that many slaveholders in the early history of the United States of America did not want their slaves
to be exposed to Christianity.[121]

Peter called on believing slaves to suffer wrongfully and
endure grief because of their "conscience toward God." In
other words, Peter did not base his appeal on a divine man-
date for slavery but on the possibility of turning a painful
but unavoidable social requirement into an opportunity for
Christian witness. God describes the willing endurance of
wrongful suffering as "commendable."

Suffering in and of itself is not "commendable to God," but
God does commend wrongful suffering "for conscience toward
God." It is, in other words, undeserved suffering for the sake of
one's Christian testimony. We must not read into this text more
than is actually there. Although the passage holds up Christ
as an example of unjust suffering that led to death, it does not
follow that believing servants must willingly die at the hands
of unscrupulous masters. Even the law of Moses recognized a
slave's right to escape from his master.[122] There is no reason to
think that if a slave's life were in danger it would be dishonor-
able for him to flee for his life. The limit of the slave's duty
was to submit willingly to unjust suffering.

To read what the biblical letters of the first century say
about suffering can be quite uncomfortable for us. First, most
of us don't enjoy suffering under any circumstance. Second,
our culture places a premium on comfort. One symptom of
this is the report that the use of the five most popular painkill-
ers increased 90 percent between 1997 and 2005.[123] Third, the
notion that people of genuine faith should be able to avoid suffering has crept into the thinking of some Christians. But it is
not helpful to deny the reality of suffering or to claim it has no
place in the Christian life. Suffering arrives in our lives from a

variety of sources. But the Bible lets us know that God is with us in our suffering, that He will sustain us through the most difficult times if we will trust in Him, and that it is even possible our suffering can be an occasion for our faith in Christ to shine so brightly that others will be drawn to faith in him.

In chapter 14, we will read further in Peter's first letter to examine what he had to say about suffering. As challenging as it is for us, we will learn that it is sometimes the will of God for believers to suffer. And we will learn how we are to respond when this is the case.

14
Suffering According to God's Will

In chapter 13 we talked about the ongoing and increasing problem of the persecution and even martyrdom of Christians around the world. We also began to look at what Peter said about suffering among Christians during the first century. We saw that believers should rejoice greatly in the face of various trials because these trials prove the genuineness of faith and assure that our faith will be found to praise, honor, and glory at the revelation of Jesus Christ. We also saw that first-century servants who had placed their faith in Jesus Christ were to submit to their masters, whether their masters were good and gentle or harsh. Peter wrote that "when you do good and suffer, if you take it patiently, this is commendable before God" (I Peter 2:20). Peter offered the ultimate example of Jesus Christ, who did good and yet suffered.

The central theme of Peter's first letter is the appropriate Christian response to suffering. Now, we will look at what Peter said about this in the rest of his letter. First, notice how Peter echoed the words of the prophet Isaiah.

Who is he who will harm you if you become followers of what is good? But even if you should suffer for righteousness'

161

sake, you are blessed. "And do not be afraid of their threats, nor be troubled." But sanctify the Lord God in your hearts, and always be ready to give a defense to everyone who asks you a reason of the hope that is in you, with meekness and fear; having a good conscience, that when they defame you as evildoers, those who revile your good conduct in Christ may be ashamed. For it is better, if it is the will of God, to suffer for doing good than for doing evil (I Peter 3:13-17).

To this point in his first letter, Peter has alluded several times to the possibility of suffering for one's faith. Beginning here, he dealt specifically and at length not only with the possibility of suffering for one's faith in Christ but also with the proper response a believer should have to suffering. This response would ideally lead the persecutor to faith in Christ.

According to Peter, believers can face persecution boldly for four reasons. First, those who persecute them will ultimately be ashamed.[124] Second, it is better to suffer for doing good than for doing evil.[125] Third, Christ offered an example of suffering.[126] Fourth, those who persecute Christians will answer to God.[127]

First Peter 3:13 suggests that if believers follow what is good, they have less likelihood of being harmed. Although the next verse acknowledges the possibility of persecution, verse 13 indicates that when Christians do good they reduce the probability of being abused because of their faith. We see the reason for the lessened probability of persecution in the specific definition of the "good" here. Contextually, to do "good" is to seek and pursue peace. Those who seek peace with others minimize the potential of conflict.

However, as I Peter 3:14 points out, a person who pursues peace in all relationships still faces the possibility of suffering "for righteousness' sake." As it turned out historically for the first-century church, a period of persecution was just around the corner.

Contrary to what might seem true to human senses, those who suffer for righteousness' sake are blessed. The usual sense of the Greek word translated "blessed" is that the person is the "privileged recipient of divine favor."[128] It is a privilege to suffer for one's faith, for those who suffer will receive a great reward in Heaven. In addition, their suffering allows them to stand in solidarity with the great Hebrew prophets, according to the words of Jesus in the Sermon on the Mount.[129]

To suffer "for righteousness' sake" is to suffer for doing right. In the context of Peter's letter, this means to suffer for believing in Jesus Christ and for the lifestyle that arises out of faith in Him.

Peter's appeal to Isaiah 8:12 was meant to encourage his readers not to fear those who threaten them. In their original context, Isaiah's words, "Do not be afraid of their threats, nor be troubled," are part of his warnings about Assyria's imminent invasion of Samaria. Rather than advising his hearers to fear Assyria, Isaiah said, "The Lord of hosts, Him you shall hallow; let Him be your fear, and let Him be your dread" (Isaiah 8:13). This passage was appropriate for Peter's use. Believers could be threatened by unbelievers—just as the people of Samaria were threatened by Assyria—but the proper response is not to join them or even to fear them. The proper response is to keep one's faith in God. First Peter 3:15 describes this response more fully.

When faced with persecution for their faith, believers should respond first by sanctifying the Lord God in their hearts. The word translated "sanctify" ordinarily refers to setting something apart or someone apart as holy, but here it means to treat the Lord God as holy or regard Him reverently. In view of their origin in Isaiah 8:13, these words indicate that those who face persecution should remember God is in control, not those who persecute them.

163

The second response believers should have when they face persecution for their faith is to "be ready to give a defense to everyone who asks . . . a reason for the hope that is in you." In the larger context of the letter, the believer's conduct toward unbelievers opens the door to the possibility that unbelievers will ask them the reason for their hope. Even in the midst of persecution, the believer's conduct can be pleasant. In this way, persecution would inevitably lead to the further growth of the church.

The curiosity of unbelievers will be piqued when they observe the believers' hope. Compared with the unbelieving world at large, there is something unusual about believers' life and values. Their hope arises out of Christ's resurrection and the way His resurrection guarantees their eternal reward. Their hope is based on the future appearing of Jesus Christ. This hope will always clearly identify those who are believers, for apart from Christ there is no hope in this world. As we progress toward the fulfillment of the prophecies concerning the decay of human civilization, the hope we embrace will become even more vivid in contrast to the hopelessness of a society without Christ.

Christians are to offer their defense of their hope with "meekness and fear." There is no place for arrogance in Christian witness. Meekness has to do with gentleness. Fear is reverence for God, not terror of people. As believers respond to the questions of unbelievers, their gentleness and reverence for God must be evident to those who hear them. These qualities alone are very persuasive in a society where arrogance and harshness are common and where people often disregard or mock God.

As Christians respond to persecution, they must do so with a good conscience. In other words, there must be no basis in truth for the evil that critics speak against them. The evil that is spoken against them must be completely false. If believers are to be defamed, it must be for their "good conduct in Christ."

164

Although, according to I Peter 3:13, those who are "followers of what is good" minimize the probability of being persecuted, verse 17 indicates that it may sometimes be the will of God for a believer to suffer for doing good. Spiritual benefits arise from suffering in the will of God when we accept that suffering and recognize it as God's instrument in working out some good thing. Suffering tends to purify our motives; it helps us reorient our priorities and reassess our values.

The discussion of suffering continues in I Peter 4:1. Again, Peter held up Christ as the example: "Therefore, since Christ suffered for us in the flesh, arm yourselves also with the same mind, for he who has suffered in the flesh has ceased from sin." The idea of "arming" oneself is a military metaphor. Craig Keener points out that the term describes believers as "arming, training, or otherwise preparing themselves for battle and possible death. The sense seems to be that those who died with Christ through faith . . . are genuinely prepared to suffer with him in any other way, including martyrdom."[130]

To arm oneself "with the same mind" as Christ had regarding His suffering means to be willing to accept unjust suffering as part of God's larger plan by which He works out His purposes. A simple attitude shift cannot develop this mindset. To genuinely think as Christ, we must be sincerely convinced that suffering is an instrument in the hands of God that will ultimately bring good things to pass.

A major section of Peter's teaching concerning suffering is found later in the fourth chapter of I Peter.

Beloved, do not think it strange concerning the fiery trial which is to try you, as though some strange thing happened to you; but rejoice to the extent that you partake of Christ's sufferings, that when His glory is revealed, you may also

165

be glad with exceeding joy. If you are reproached for the name of Christ, blessed are you, for the Spirit of glory and of God rests upon you. On their part He is blasphemed, but on your part He is glorified. But let none of you suffer as a murderer, a thief, an evildoer, or as a busybody in other people's matters. Yet if anyone suffers as a Christian, let him not be ashamed, but let him glorify God in this matter. For the time has come for judgment to begin at the house of God; and if it begins with us first, what will be the end of those who do not obey the gospel of God? Now "If the righteous one is scarcely saved, where will the ungodly and the sinner appear?" Therefore let those who suffer according to the will of God commit their souls to Him in doing good, as to a faithful Creator (I Peter 4:12-19).

In this discussion of suffering, Peter explained that our response to trials should not be surprise, but rejoicing. We must be certain there is no basis for our suffering in wrongdoing.

In I Peter 4:12, Peter returned to the idea of fiery trials, which he first mentioned in I Peter 1:7. The idea is that just as fire purges the impurities from precious metals, so the fiery trials of believers have a cleansing effect. They come specifically to "try us," a phrase that refers to putting us to the test. Substantial biblical evidence confirms that God may allow painful circumstances to come into our lives in order to accomplish some greater good. But this good is accomplished only as we respond to suffering with faith and by committing ourselves to God.

We should not be surprised to experience fiery trials. It has always been the experience of people of faith who are, as Peter says, strangers in this world to be ridiculed and rejected by those who do not understand them. Christ Himself was the supreme example of this, and those who identify with Him will tend to be treated as He was.

According to I Peter 4:13, a believer's right response to suffering is to rejoice because of the way suffering identifies him with Christ. In similar statements in the Sermon on the Mount, Jesus described the blessed state of those who are persecuted for the sake of righteousness. Those who suffer for doing right are blessed because the kingdom of Heaven is theirs and because they have a great reward in Heaven. Their persecution identifies them with the Hebrew prophets in their suffering.

The Greco-Roman society of the first century was obsessed with shame and honor. The idea that it was noble to suffer ridicule for doing good would have shocked those who embraced the ideals of that culture.[131] But biblical values are often at odds with those of society at large.

Believers are human, and it is sometimes difficult to maintain the right attitude in the painful circumstances of life. But focusing on faith's ultimate reward can help the believer to keep the right perspective. Peter said believers can rejoice in the face of suffering as they anticipate even greater gladness at the revelation of Christ's glory.

First Peter 4:14 indicates that reproach itself is not a cause for joy, but one's identification with Christ is cause for joy. Peter referred to being reproached "for the name of Christ." In Hebrew thought, the idea of "name" was much more than a label. Instead, "name" was virtually equivalent with "person." "Name" could also signify character, reputation, works, and worth. To be reproached for the "name of Christ" means to suffer reproach for the "person of Christ."

The reason believers are blessed in the midst of suffering is that "the spirit of glory and of God" rests on those who are reproached for Christ. The previous verse indicates that the glory to which Peter referred is the glory of Christ that will be revealed at His coming. Even now, the spirit of that glory rests on those who believe in Him.

Next, Peter declared that believers should not suffer for wrongdoing. He gave a short list of prohibited behavior, lumping busybodies together with murderers and thieves. This list is no doubt intended to represent all activities Christians should avoid.

Then we learn that if any believer suffers because of his identification with Christ, he should not be ashamed. Rather, he should view the suffering as an occasion to glorify, or to praise and worship God. It may come as quite a surprise to us, but Peter's use of the word "Christian" in the phrase "if anyone suffers as a Christian" is one of only three times the word "Christian" appears in the New Testament. First, unbelievers used it to describe those who follow Christ.[132] Next, an unbelieving civil ruler, Agrippa, used it to describe Paul's attempt to bring him into agreement with those who believe on Christ.[133] Peter used the word to describe the perspective of unbelievers who justify their persecution of believers by identifying them as Christians.

The word "Christian" means something like "those of Christ's party," just as the word "Herodian" describes those who were aligned with Herod's coalition. In this case, to suffer for the charge of being a Christian is parallel to suffering for the charge of being a murderer, a thief, an evildoer, or a busybody in other men's matters. Although we have come to treasure the identification "Christian," those who first used the term never intended it to be a compliment. Because of what was at that time the derogatory nature of the term, Peter urged believers not to be ashamed for any suffering that arises from identification with Christ. Contrary to the opinion of those who would persecute Christians for their faith, it is not shameful to be identified with Christ. To be so closely identified with Him as to suffer for that reason is cause to praise and worship God.

In this series of verses addressing the problem of suffering, the last verse states that suffering can be the will of God.

Peter wrote, "Therefore let those who suffer according to the will of God commit their souls to Him in doing good, as to a faithful Creator" (I Peter 4:19). The point is that since the difficulty of fiery trials is a consequence of one's faith in God and the suffering associated with these trials is "according to the will of God," believers who experience this suffering should respond by committing their souls to God and demonstrating this commitment by doing good. Even in the face of suffering we must continue to do the right thing.

Peter's perspective here is the same as Paul's. Paul learned that his "thorn in the flesh" was an instrument in the hands of God to prevent him from being "exalted above measure." Near the end of his first letter, Peter's last reference to suffering assured, "May the God of all grace, who called us to His eternal glory by Christ Jesus, after you have suffered a while, perfect, establish, strengthen, and settle you" (I Peter 5:10). The glory to which we are called is eternal; the suffering we endure is just for a while. This temporary suffering will result in the perfecting, establishing, strengthening, and settling of those who believe.

The word translated "perfect" is often used in the New Testament with the idea of mending or repairing something that has been broken. That seems to be the point here. It may be the will of God for believers to suffer temporarily, but the suffering will be followed by restoration and mending of whatever may have been broken during the suffering.

The word "establish" has to do with something being strengthened or made firm. Since the next word in the list specifically describes strengthening, perhaps we should take this to refer specifically to making something firm. In the context of suffering, this seems to be a promise that God will firmly establish those who have suffered to any degree that they have experienced loss by their suffering.

169

The word translated "strengthen" involves making something strong, with specific application to the soul. God will remove any weakness that may have resulted from suffering.

Finally, the word "settle" has to do with laying a foundation or making something stable. Thus, if any believer's stability has been damaged by suffering, God will correct it.

Notice how this verse is connected with the preceding verse. It contrasts grammatically with I Peter 5:9, which describes the spiritual struggle in which believers are engaged. First Peter 5:8-9 warns that we as believers should "be sober, be vigilant; because [our] adversary the devil walks about like a roaring lion, seeking whom he may devour. [We should] resist him, steadfast in the faith, knowing that the same sufferings are experienced by [our] brotherhood in the world." When we follow these words with those found next in I Peter 5:10, we discover that although believers are now locked in spiritual battle with the devil, the day is coming when that will be over and any painful results of that war will be removed. We may suffer now, but we have the assurance that at the end of our suffering we will be perfected, established, strengthened, and settled.

In the following chapters, we will discuss other dimensions of the human problem of suffering. But for now, we should embrace our solidarity with first-century Christians, our spiritual forebears who learned how to rejoice when they suffered for their faith in Christ. This suffering came from many directions, even from within their families. But they discovered that to be persecuted for Christ's sake was a glorious honor with an assurance of an eternal reward. May our Lord help us, in the midst of our pain, to keep eternity's values in view.

15
Suffering as a Victim

In its ethical position paper on suffering, the Christian Medical and Dental Society offers the following explanation.

> Suffering occurs when we perceive or actually experience a threat to or loss of our wholeness. Wholeness includes an individual's cognitive, emotional, spiritual, and physical conditions, which are inherently interrelated. While pain is [an] important component of suffering, it may sometimes protect us. Suffering may even provide an opportunity to experience God's grace.
>
> Suffering has a variety of causes and effects. Suffering may be the result of personal choices, or other's choices, or may come without obvious reason or explanation. Everyone suffers; particular instances of suffering are not necessarily the result of spiritual or moral failure. Suffering may compel us to confront the meaning and purpose of our existence and to question the goodness and justice or even the existence of God.[134]

In the preceding chapters, we've discussed many of these ideas. We have determined that suffering has various causes, including personal choices and choices made by other people, and that sometimes there is no apparent reason.

Now let's talk about the problem of victimization. What does the Bible say about the possibility that people can be victims of bad choices made by others? If we stop and think about this for a moment, we recognize that Scripture has a great deal to say about this. Many Bible stories are about people who suffered for no immediately apparent reason. Whether the subject is Joseph's betrayal by his brothers and his subsequent imprisonment, Saul's persecution of David, or other events like these, it seems that much of the Old Testament consists of stories of those who suffered in innocence. In some cases—like Joseph's—the Bible tells us God was involved in the suffering in order to bring some good thing to pass. As Joseph said to his brothers after the death of their father, "You meant evil against me; but God meant it for good, in order to bring it about as it is this day, to save many people alive" (Genesis 50:20). Surely there were many times before Joseph's promotion in Egypt that he wondered why he had experienced such pain. Think of how Joseph must have felt when his brothers threatened him with death, cast him into a pit, and sold him as a slave. He was lied on for resisting temptation, cast into prison, and forgotten by those whom he had helped at their time of need. Although God had given Joseph dreams about his future, Joseph had no way of knowing how or when they would be fulfilled. Can a dream survive betrayal? Can a dream live in a pit and in a prison? Can slaves hold on to their dreams?

Not every story of suffering in the Bible ends like Joseph's. Although it is very possible for a morning of joy to follow a night of weeping for those who trust God in the midst of their suffering, that morning of joy does not always dawn on this earth. Many people suffer without ever knowing why, and, for

172

many of them, their suffering ends only in death. This is not just negative thinking; it is reality. Does the Bible offer any help to those who suffer for no apparent reason? Does God's sovereignty mean He controls everything that happens? Must we think God is behind every painful event that life brings our way? Can we trust and love a God who intentionally hurts us, even if He does intend to bring something good out of our pain somewhere down the road?

Questions like these make us uncomfortable. Even worse is the idea that every happening is the will of God in the sense that God is the one who caused the event. Is God's will always done? Peter wrote, "The Lord is . . . not willing that any should perish but that all should come to repentance" (II Peter 3:9). Yet all do not come to repentance. There are some who perish. Accepting the idea that God's will is not always done releases us from the spiritual and emotional trauma that results from trying to understand and explain horrendous acts of evil and violence, destructive accidents, or even what we may call "acts of nature." The latter—involving things like floods, famines, fires, earthquakes, and hurricanes—are often called "acts of God."

In previous chapters, we acknowledged that God can do anything He wishes, but we also saw that God has chosen to limit Himself within the parameters of what it means for His creation to be what it is. This means, for example, that since God created human beings in His image, we are able to choose and act freely and God will not stop us. For God to control our choices would be to violate His creative act of making us creatures with freedom of choice. This can clearly be seen in Genesis 3. Although God had warned Adam not to eat of the tree of the knowledge of good and evil, He did not intervene to prevent Adam from disobeying His command. The history of the human race is the history of people making free choices,

173

often with disastrous consequences for themselves or others.

What about the rest of creation? Has sin negatively impacted nature? Paul addressed this issue in Romans 8:19-22.

> For the earnest expectation of the creation eagerly waits for the revealing of the sons of God. For the creation was subjected to futility, not willingly, but because of Him who subjected it in hope; because the creation itself also will be delivered from the bondage of corruption into the glorious liberty of the children of God. For we know that the whole creation groans and labors with birth pangs together until now (Romans 8:19-22).

The corruption sin introduced into the realm of creation was not limited to the human race; the effects of sin impacted all of creation. According to Genesis 3:17-19, the ground produces thorns and thistles because it has been cursed. The creation of a new universe is necessary because sin infected the entire created realm. Isaiah wrote, "Behold, I create new heavens and a new earth; and the former shall not be remembered or come to mind" (Isaiah 65:17). The Lord said the new heavens and the new earth would remain.[135] Peter referred to this when he wrote his vision of the future.

> The day of the Lord will come as a thief in the night, in which the heavens will pass away with a great noise, and the elements will melt with fervent heat; both the earth and the works that are in it will be burned up. Therefore, since all these things will be dissolved, what manner of persons ought you to be in holy conduct and godliness, looking for and hastening the coming of the day of God, because of which the heavens will be dissolved, being

174

on fire, and the elements will melt with fervent heat? Nevertheless we, according to His promise, look for new heavens and a new earth in which righteousness dwells (II Peter 3:10-13).

We are not yet living in that new heavens and new earth; the universe in which we live still struggles with the consequences of corruption brought on by the fall of the human race. Since that is true, we shouldn't be too quick to blame God for natural disasters.

Although we may not completely understand why or how sin infected the natural realm, we should hesitate to attribute famine, starvation, floods, earthquakes, and destructive winds to God. Although the point of the story is not to address the fallenness of creation, the prophet Elijah's encounter with the destructive forces of nature does seem instructive. As Elijah stood on a mountain, "a great and strong wind tore into the mountains and broke the rocks in pieces before the Lord, but the Lord was not in the wind; and after the wind an earthquake, but the Lord was not in the earthquake; and after the earthquake a fire, but the Lord was not in the fire" (I Kings 19:11-12). When all of these natural phenomena subsided, Elijah heard God speak in a still, small voice. (See I Kings 19:12.)

Some time ago, at a camp meeting, I spoke on the subject of suffering. After the lessons, several people shared their stories with me. They were heartfelt and sensitive accounts of personal struggle ranging from battles with disease to broken families. One pastor told me of his attempt to minister to a person who had lost family members in an automobile accident. When he asked God what to say, Ecclesiastes 9:11 came to his mind. This verse reads, "I returned and saw under the sun that—the race is not to the swift, nor the battle to the strong,

175

nor bread to the wise, nor riches to men of understanding, nor favor to men of skill; but time and chance happen to them all." The next verse continues, "For man also does not know his time: like fish taken in a cruel net, like birds caught in a snare, so the sons of men are snared in an evil time, when it falls suddenly upon them" (Ecclesiastes 9:12).

Was this pastor right to think that the best explanation for an automobile accident was that "time and chance" happen to everyone? I believe so. I can't bring myself to believe God caused the automobile accident and the resulting deaths. If we must have a reason, we could say that perhaps someone was careless, speeding, or intoxicated. If not this, perhaps one of the automobiles had a leaking seal on the steering column or worn brake pads. If not this, maybe the roadway was poorly designed. Someone could even have caused the wreck intentionally. But none of these is a reason to accuse God.

Someone may ask why God did not supernaturally intervene to prevent the accident. Certainly God could do that and sometimes does. We've all heard stories about miraculous deliverances from what appeared to be certain disaster. My wife and I have such a story to tell, and you may too. But the fact that God can intervene does not mean He always does so. If He did, not only would the word "miracle" lose its meaning, but freedom of choice would be nonexistent and the universe would be reduced to a machine manipulated by God like we manipulate vending machines. It would be a soulless and mindless world, devoid of meaning, no more significant than the toy soldiers used by a boy in his play. This is not the kind of world God created, and God cannot be blamed for the corruption and decay introduced into His creation when human beings exercised free choice. If God had not given human beings freedom of choice, creation would have started out as plastic toy soldiers.

The idea that some things happen simply by chance is not just Solomon's opinion as recorded in the Book of Ecclesiastes. Notice how Jesus responded when He heard the news that Pilate had killed some people along with the animals they had planned to sacrifice.

> There were present at that season some who told Him about the Galileans whose blood Pilate had mingled with their sacrifices. And Jesus answered and said to them, "Do you suppose that these Galileans were worse sinners than all other Galileans, because they suffered such things? I tell you no; but unless you repent you will all likewise perish. Or those eighteen on whom the tower in Siloam fell and killed them, do you think that they were worse sinners than all other men who dwelt in Jerusalem? I tell you, no; but unless you repent you will all likewise perish" (Luke 13:1-5).

Here are two very different situations, both of which resulted in pain and suffering. The first involves victims of Pilate, by whose authorization these people were killed along with their sacrificial animals. The second case does not involve people hurting other people, but an event we would call an accident. As these individuals walked near a tower, it toppled and killed eighteen of them. In both cases, Jesus asked whether those who suffered did so because they were worse sinners than others. Was God meting out judgment on these people because of their sins? No. Their sin had not caused their suffering. Although everyone who does not repent will eventually perish, these people died for two different reasons. The first group died because Pilate wanted them to die. The second group died because they were in the wrong place at the wrong time.

These two situations serve to represent many of the episodes of suffering we experience. These people did not die because of God's judgment for their sins. They did not die because of some cosmic encounter like the one behind Job's suffering. They did not die to prevent them from being puffed up because of the abundant revelations they had received, like Paul. The first group died by Pilate's decree. They were his victims. The second group may have died because the ancient Tower of Siloam had shifted on its foundation. In chapter 16, we will deal with the problem of accidents. But for now, let's consider the problem of victimization.

The fact that human beings have the ability to love means they also have the ability to hate. It follows that the ability to be kind is also the ability to be cruel, and the ability to nurse a person back to health is also the ability to kill that person. Since human beings can exercise their freedom of choice to do whatever they wish, and since this freedom is often exercised in selfish, arrogant, greedy, and violent ways, they abuse their freedoms and victimize others.

Some people are quick to say we should never acknowledge being a victim; we should confess only that we are victors. Those who think this way also claim we should never confess to being sick, or in pain, or suffering, or in need. Of course we must move past a mindset of victimization; we cannot wallow in our suffering. But before we can move ahead, we must first acknowledge our pain. To deny the reality of our experiences and our circumstances is counterproductive and deceptive. Although we can never compare our suffering with His, we must admit that Jesus acknowledged His pain and suffering on the cross. In the words of Psalm 22:1, Jesus prayed, "My God, My God, why have you forsaken Me?" By praying these words, Jesus claimed all of the words of the prayer found in Psalm 22 as His own. With astounding precision, the psalm prophetically records the words of those who passed by the cross, mocking Jesus.[136] It includes the words, "They pierced My hands and My feet" (Psalm 22:16). It declares, "They divide My garments among them, and for My clothing they cast lots" (Psalm 22:18). The Book of Hebrews quotes Psalm 22:22 as the words of Jesus.[137] In view of the fact that the psalm is without question a prophetic anticipation of the experiences of Jesus on the cross, we should note how the psalm reveals the Messiah's confession of His suffering. Listen again to the opening verse, then to a selection of other verses from the prayer, and ask yourself if Jesus acknowledged His suffering.

> My God, My God, why have You forsaken Me? Why are You so far from helping Me, and from the words of My groaning? O My God, I cry in the daytime, but You do not hear; and in the night season, and am not silent. . . . I am a worm, and no man; a reproach of men, and despised by the people. All those who see Me ridicule Me; . . . Many bulls have surrounded Me; . . . They gape at Me with their mouths, like a raging and roaring lion. I am poured out like water, and all My bones are out of joint; My heart is like wax; it has melted within Me. My strength is dried up like a potsherd, and My tongue clings to My jaws; You have brought Me to the dust of death (Psalm 22:1-15).

Not only do these verses reveal something of the intense suffering Jesus experienced on the cross, but as the words of His prayer, they also show us He did not deny His pain. By owning His pain and suffering, He was finally able to say, "You have answered Me. I will declare Your name to My brethren; in the midst of the assembly I will praise You" (Psalm 22:21-22). His deliverance, which did not come in the form of being spared the experience of death but in His resurrection from the dead, followed His acknowledgement and ownership of His suffering.

Perhaps someone would deny the relevance of Jesus' experience as an example for us. Maybe Jesus was willing to acknowledge His suffering because of the unique purpose for His suffering. Now that He has suffered on our behalf and redeemed us, perhaps we should no longer confess the reality of any suffering in our lives. But no, you can see a similar pattern in Paul's life. He acknowledged his suffering, his stripes, his imprisonment, his stoning, the perils he faced, his weariness, sleeplessness, hunger, thirst, his lack of adequate clothing.[138]

A great deal of the suffering we experience is the result of other people's bad decisions. It is simply wrong to deny the reality of our pain, and it is wrong to deny the pain of others. To deny the reality of pain caused by those who have victimized us is to dismiss the significance of our dignity as those who are made in God's image. Every attack on a human being is an attack on the image of God.

The significance of violent acts against a human being is seen in these words spoken after Noah's flood: "Whoever sheds man's blood, by man his blood shall be shed; for in the image of God He made man" (Genesis 9:6). The thing that makes it so wrong to attack another human being is the fact that each human being is made in the image of God. And this fact cannot be dismissed as just an Old Testament idea. In the New Testament, James wrote about the misuse of the tongue, "With [our tongue] we bless our God and Father, and with it we curse men, who have been made in the similitude of God. Out of the same mouth proceed blessing and cursing. My brethren, these things ought not to be so" (James 3:9-10). As Genesis points out, it is certainly wrong to kill a human being; people are made in the image of God. But, as James points out, it is also wrong to speak evil of human beings for the same reason. If we brush off the significance of being attacked physically or even of being cursed, we are minimizing the importance of the fact that we bear God's image. We should acknowledge our pain and suffering; in the long run, it is the only way to work through the offense in order to find release from the pain.

Every child who has been physically or sexually abused, every wife who has been beaten by a drunken or angry husband, every mother or father who has lost a son or daughter in a senseless accident, everyone who has been abandoned by an unfaithful spouse, and all who have lost loved ones to cruel diseases have wondered why those things happened. There is no need to blame God for these things, and neither must we pretend that we don't hurt. If we acknowledge our suffering, trusting God to bring us through the horror of loss, we will one day find that, like Jesus, our prayer will change from a litany of genuine expression of pain to the words, "You have answered me." The heavens will not always be silent. Our strength will not always be gone. We will experience a resurrection from the deathly experiences we have endured. And finally, we will join Christ in His resurrection, and we, like Paul, will be able to say, "Death is swallowed up in victory. O death, where is thy sting? O grave, where is thy victory?" (I Corinthians 15:54-55, KJV). No longer will we be victims. Instead, we will say, "Thanks be to God, who gives us the victory through our Lord Jesus Christ" (I Corinthians 15:57).

16
Suffering and Accidents

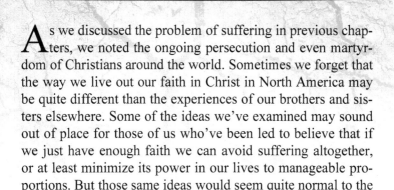

As we discussed the problem of suffering in previous chapters, we noted the ongoing persecution and even martyrdom of Christians around the world. Sometimes we forget that the way we live out our faith in Christ in North America may be quite different than the experiences of our brothers and sisters elsewhere. Some of the ideas we've examined may sound out of place for those of us who've been led to believe that if we just have enough faith we can avoid suffering altogether, or at least minimize its power in our lives to manageable proportions. But those same ideas would seem quite normal to the vast majority of Christians who live elsewhere in the world and who regularly suffer for their faith.

Ziya Meral, in her article "Bearing the Silence of God,"[139] wrote about those in the front lines who are suffering for their faith in Christ in a hostile environment.

> Statements such as, "More Christians have died for their faith in the 20th century than in all other centuries of church history combined," and, "It is estimated that two-thirds of all the martyrs in Christian history died in the 20th century," are frequently used in reports and writings on worldwide persecution today.

More Christians are killed than are saved from execution at the last minute. More Christians stay locked in prison, beaten and tortured, than are able to walk free, guided by miraculous escape plans. More Christians suffer lifelong deprivation of their most basic civic and economic rights. . . .

Above all, for the average persecuted Christian, there are unanswered prayers and the absence of peace, strength, courage, and joy. Their humanness in a very earthly plot line finds no place in our modern-day obsession with heroic stories with victorious resolutions.

If we listen carefully to these words, they ring true and express a New Testament kind of faith. There were indeed those who experienced miraculous escape from prison during the New Testament era, only to lose their lives later by crucifixion. There were many, however, who were never delivered from prison and who died in unusual and cruel ways.

At a large conference of our church some years ago, I was thrilled to hear the report of the miraculous deliverance of some of our brothers and sisters in the Philippines. The minister who gave the report held up for all to see a shirt that one of the Christians had worn during a terrorist attack on the church. The shirt was riddled with bullet holes where the terrorists had shot at the believers in an attempt to close down their meeting. The bullets penetrated the shirt—but not the body of the believer. No one was killed when the attackers threw hand grenades inside the church building. What a great, thrilling miracle it was to know that in spite of a hail of gunfire and explosives, no one in the church died!

It was not so thrilling, however, when we received news of some of our brothers and sisters in Christ who were killed during the lingering civil war in Liberia.

We are not God, and it is fruitless for us to try to second-guess Him to figure out why some are miraculously delivered and others are not. It won't do to blame those who were not delivered. The problem was not their lack of faith. As the last six verses of Hebrews 11 make clear, we can't tell by the circumstances of their lives whether or not people have faith. Those who subdued kingdoms, worked righteousness, obtained promises, stopped the mouths of lions, quenched the violence of fire, escaped the edge of the sword, out of weakness were made strong, became valiant in battle, turned to flight the armies of aliens, and received their dead raised to life again were people of faith, but so were those who were tortured, scourged, chained, imprisoned, stoned, sawn in two, tempted, slain with the sword, and who wandered about in sheepskins and goatskins, destitute, afflicted, and tormented. To say nothing negative about the heroes of faith who experienced miraculous deliverances, it is interesting that Scripture says it was those who suffered without deliverance "of whom the world was not worthy." These suffering people of faith wandered in deserts, mountains, dens, and caves of the earth. And though they obtained a good testimony through faith, they "did not receive the promise." (See Hebrews 11:32-40.)

We can see from this that faith is not simply a way to make good things happen. It does not guarantee deliverance in this world. Instead, faith enables us to trust God when deliverance does not come and when things are going from bad to worse.

As we discovered in chapter 15, some of our suffering is due to bad choices other people have made. When Jesus cited Pilate's slaughter of pilgrims from Galilee who had come to Jerusalem to offer sacrifices at the Temple, He answered, "Do you suppose that these Galileans were worse sinners than all other Galileans, because they suffered such things? I tell you, no; but unless you repent you will all likewise perish" (Luke 13:2-3). The common mindset in the first century said that when people experienced suffering it was God's punishment for their sins. It is evident that even Jesus' disciples held this view when they supposed that a man blind from birth had suffered this punishment for his parents' sins or even for the sins he himself had committed while he was still in his mother's womb. Jesus denied this way of thinking. In the case of the Galileans whom Pilate killed, it had nothing to do with their sins. It had to do, instead, with Pilate's exercise of his power of choice. These people were Pilate's victims.

We also learned in chapter 15 that we move past victimization when we acknowledge our suffering but continue to trust God in the face of our pain and questions. As Paul wrote, we can give thanks to God "who gives us the victory through our Lord Jesus Christ" (I Corinthians 15:57).

Another reason for suffering has nothing to do with punishment for our sins or intentional injury by other people. This can be seen in Jesus' continuing response to those who told Him about Pilate's treatment of the Galileans. Jesus said, "Or those eighteen on whom the tower in Siloam fell and killed them, do you think that they were worse sinners than all other men who dwelt in Jerusalem? I tell you, no; but unless you repent you will all likewise perish" (Luke 13:4-5).

Even today when tragedy strikes, some people immediately think God must be punishing those who suffer. Those who think this way are like the natives of the island of Malta. Paul, who was a prisoner aboard a ship, escaped shipwreck and washed up on a beach in Malta. He began gathering sticks for a fire when a poisonous snake sprang out of the heat and fastened onto his hand. When the natives saw the snake hanging from Paul's hand, they said, "No doubt this man is a murderer, whom, though he has escaped the sea, yet justice does not allow to live" (Acts 28:4). Of course this was not true, and Paul shook the snake off into the fire without suffering any harm. The attitude of the people of Malta is not far from the superstitions of a bygone era when people would knock on wood in hopes of preventing some bad thing from happening, or avoid crossing the path of a black cat, walking under a ladder, or opening an umbrella indoors.

But since we are not perfect, we can expect our imperfections to have consequences. Many years ago, during my last year in college, I worked for a company that manufactured windows for automobiles. The company implemented a program called Zero Defects. It was a noble—but impossible—goal to produce absolutely perfect glass. Nothing that is produced by imperfect human beings can be consistently perfect. We discarded a great deal of glass in that plant, and I still have two scars from my attempts to participate in that ambitious but hopeless endeavor. I'm sure our efforts reduced the amount of flawed glass in those sixties-model cars, but it's very possible some of those cars are still being driven today with their flawed windows intact. It's possible some of those windows cracked or even exploded, as the rear window did on a car I owned some years ago.

If someone finds imperfect glass in his car, should he blame God? This question sounds trivial until we realize many of the car accidents experienced every day, even those that result in permanent injury or death, are the result of some error—however slight—made by someone who was not as careful as he should have been. Maybe he didn't tighten the steering mechanism sufficiently as the car passed him in the assembly line. Or if the assembly was done by a robot, perhaps the person responsible for the robot's performance was a bit

187

careless in making the adjustments or settings that were needed to assure that the steering mechanism was properly installed. Then, the attention of the person responsible for quality control may have been briefly diverted at a critical moment, so that the error was not noticed.

All of this may sound like speculation, but it is not. Many have lost control of their automobiles because of steering defects, causing not only their crash but others as well. Many accidents happen because car owners do not properly maintain their vehicles or because they drive while sleepy or because they are talking on a cell phone, fiddling with the sound system, smoking a cigarette, or just carrying on a conversation with other passengers.

Can God be blamed for these things? Of course not. Nor can we say events like these are God's judgment on those who suffer because of human carelessness or incompetence.

Jesus felt keenly enough about what is and what is not signified by accidents that He told the story about the eighteen people who were killed when the Tower of Siloam fell on them. The reason He told this story was to reveal the error in the thinking of those who believe such events were engineered by God as judgment upon these eighteen people. Jesus specifically denied this. The collapse of the Tower of Siloam and the fact that they happened to be standing beneath it or passing by at that moment had nothing to do with their sins. These people may have been killed only because the mortar holding the stones in place became dry and cracked. If mortar was not used, it was either some other defect in construction or the settling of the earth that caused the stones in the tower to come loose, plummet to the earth, and strike their victims. If we knew those eighteen people personally, we would probably find that they represented a cross section of the population of first-century Israel. No doubt there were all kinds of people who died, from all walks of life, old and young, rich and poor, godly and ungodly.

According to Jesus, there is one thing for sure. No one could rightly blame God for the collapse of the tower. These kinds of things happen today. Just a few weeks before I wrote this, I heard the news that an old satellite was falling to earth. Because of the concern for where it might land, and also because it carried a substance that would be harmful to human beings, the United States government decided to try to destroy the satellite before it crashed to the earth. I suppose we escaped any problem there, but we regularly hear of parts falling off airplanes and hurtling through the roofs of homes. Meteorites sometimes do the same thing. Can we blame God for this? No, we are the ones who send up the satellites, knowing that what goes up must come down, and we are the ones who decide to build our homes where we do and the way we do.

If we are to deal successfully with the traumatic events of life, we must accept personal responsibility for our actions and refuse to blame others, including God, who had nothing to do with the event. If someone was involved in hurting us, like Pilate with the Galileans, it is right and good to hold that person responsible for his actions. If we think it is wrong to do this, we would have to say it will be wrong for God to hold every human being responsible for the deeds they have done. Paul wrote, however, that God will "render to each one according to his deeds" (Romans 2:6). We may assume that since we are not God, and since we ourselves are imperfect, we should not hold others accountable for their actions, even if they have injured us. If so, we would be wrong. The apostle John held those who had attacked him responsible for what they had done. He said, "I wrote to the church, but Diotrephes, who loves to have the preeminence among them, does not receive us. Therefore, if I come, I will call to mind his deeds which he does, prating against us with malicious words. And not content with that, he himself does not receive the brethren, and forbids those who wish to, putting them out of the church" (III John 9-10). John is not the only first-century believer who held people responsible for what they had done.

So if we want to respond in a God-honoring way to our pain and suffering, what should we do? Here's a list of suggested responses based on what we have learned to this point.

1. Don't waste time asking why. We will rarely be able to answer that question correctly. But even if we did discover the reason for our suffering, it would not solve our problem or make the suffering easier to bear.
2. Don't waste time with intense introspection. If you did do something that caused your pain, you will know that without examining and reexamining every thought you've ever had and everything you've ever done. Martin Luther tried to deal with his emotional trauma by confessing his sins by the hour, and the distress drove him to the brink of insanity. Only when he discovered that peace comes from faith was his life transformed.
3. Don't ask "what if." It is quite common for people to respond to suffering by speculating about what would have happened under other circumstances. If only they had left the house ten minutes earlier . . . if only they had taken another route . . . if only they had driven the other car . . . if only they had seen the doctor earlier. There is no point in this. What has been done can't be undone. We must take things as they are, regardless of

how they got that way. We cannot undo the past; we can affect only the future.

4. Don't blame God. The chances are that God had nothing to do with causing your suffering. But if He did, as in the case of Job or Paul, we can be sure He has a purpose in what He does. We will discover, like Job, the Lord is very compassionate and merciful. As Job said, when He has tested us, we will come forth as gold.[140]

5. Trust God. If God is behind your trial, He will bring you through it. But if He is not behind it, He is still God and He is able to work out His eternal purposes regardless of what people do. Remember the analogy of the chess game. God not only knows the next move each person will make, He knows every conceivable move that could be made at each point in the game. Even though He gives each person freedom to choose every move, God is able to move in such a way as to bring the game to the conclusion He has in view. This does not mean God will force any person to be saved or lost, but it does mean He will do whatever needs to be done to ensure that everything works together—including each bad move—for the good of those who love Him, who are the called according to His purpose.[141]

The good news is, no matter whether your pain is because you've been someone's victim, or whether you've suffered from some chance accident, or whether it is simply the unexplained choice of the sovereign God, your suffering does not mean God no longer loves you. Paul wrote to the suffering church at Rome to assure them of God's love.

For I consider that the sufferings of this present time are not worthy to be compared with the glory which shall be revealed in us. . . . Who shall separate us from the love of Christ? Shall tribulation, or distress, or persecution, or famine, or nakedness, or peril, or sword? . . . Yet in all these things we are more than conquerors through Him who loved us. For I am persuaded that neither death nor life, nor angels nor principalities nor powers, nor things present nor things to come, nor height nor depth, nor any other created thing, shall be able to separate us from the love of God which is in Christ Jesus our Lord (Romans 8:18, 35, 37-39).

Paul's point isn't that we will never experience these painful circumstances, but that we probably will. Even if we do, none of these things indicate that God does not love us. These things happen because we live in an imperfect world among imperfect people. But in the midst of our pain we can say, like Paul, "If God is for us, who can be against us?" (Romans 8:31). It's not that no one can be against us, but that it doesn't matter who or what is against us. Since God is for us, the efforts of those who are against us are in vain. In the end, their destructive purposes for our lives will not prevail. God's purposes will.

So trust God in your pain! In the world to come, which is the only world that really matters, you will not hunger or thirst anymore, for the Lamb who is in the midst of the throne will feed you and lead you to living fountains of waters, and God will wipe away every tear from your eyes.[142]

17
Embracing Suffering as a Friend

In this chapter, I would like for us to think about the possibility of embracing suffering as a friend. This may at first seem like a radical idea. Why would anyone want to think of suffering as a friend? We tend to put a premium on being pain free. We don't like pain, and we don't like problems we can't solve quickly. This view of life has given birth to a multibillion-dollar industry in potions and elixirs that promise to free us from pain and in self-help books that offer the promise of a quick fix for all of life's problems.

But the truth is that the human experience is an experience of suffering. This is a consequence of the Fall in the Garden of Eden, and it will not be reversed until we enter the eternal state. From beginning to end, the biblical story is of godly men and women who learned to trust God even when it hurts.

I want us to think about embracing suffering as a friend because, from a biblical perspective, suffering should be an occasion for rejoicing, not for questioning God or for giving up hope. Let's think seriously about some of the biblical insights on suffering. Paul wrote to the believers in Rome: "We also glory in tribulations, knowing that tribulation produces perseverance; and perseverance, character; and character, hope.

Now hope does not disappoint, because the love of God has been poured out in our hearts by the Holy Spirit who was given to us" (Romans 5:3-5). We are to glory in tribulation because it produces perseverance. The King James Version translates this as "tribulation worketh patience."

I am a third-generation preacher of the gospel. The first preacher in our family was my grandfather, L. D. Segraves. He was an "old time" preacher, and he believed in taking the Bible literally. Once when a woman in the church asked him to pray for her that God would give her patience, my grandfather began to pray, "Oh, Lord, I pray that you would send this woman tribulation!" She said, "No, I don't want tribulation; I want patience!" My grandfather responded, "But the Bible says that tribulation worketh patience!"

As amusing as this may be, my grandfather was on to something. The Bible does indeed say tribulation produces patience, or perseverance. The point is, some character qualities are developed only in the midst of suffering. These qualities can't be known by living a pain-free, problem-free life. Literally, the Greek word translated "tribulation" means "pressure." It is as we respond in faith to the pressures of life that we develop patience, one of the most valuable virtues. To respond in faith means, according to Paul, we glory in tribulation or in pressure. We actually welcome it into our lives, knowing it will produce in us something of such lasting and significant value that it will cause us to forget the suffering we endured to obtain it.

This does not mean we go out searching for suffering. Life itself will produce plenty of opportunities for us to glory in tribulations without our seeking them out. But it does mean that when trouble comes, we embrace the potential it has to develop character in us so long as we keep our faith in God, trusting Him regardless of life's circumstances. In the final analysis, what other option do we have? We can rail against our pain or pretend it isn't there, but these are not solutions to the problem. To glory in it involves facing it head-on and acknowledging its impact on us, while at the same time looking for ways to turn pressure into patience. This will, of course, involve talking to God about it and probably discussing it with wise and mature people who have already learned how to grow through suffering.

It seems that Paul and James were on the same page concerning the value of suffering for developing character. James wrote, "My brethren, count it all joy when you fall into various trials, knowing that the testing of your faith produces patience. But let patience have its perfect work, that you may be perfect and complete, lacking nothing" (James 1:2-4). Paul said we should glory in tribulation. James said we should count it all joy when we confront trials. Both Paul and James saw the potential of developing patience if we respond to trouble in the right way. James seems to be saying that we should not look for a quick fix; we should let patience have its perfect work. In other words, we're not in a hurry to put the problem behind us; we welcome the problem, examining it for its ability to help us reorient our priorities and to look at life and at our relationship with God from a more mature perspective. The way James put it, it may be impossible to be perfect and complete, lacking nothing, without embracing the positive potential of suffering.

The people of great faith in the Bible were people who knew how to rejoice in suffering, how to embrace it as a friend. David wrote, "It is good for me that I have been afflicted, that I may learn Your statutes" (Psalm 119:71). Apparently David's ability to truly learn God's laws would have been minimized if he had not experienced affliction.

195

In addition to the words of Paul we have looked at in previous chapters, he also made the following observations about suffering.

We are hard pressed on every side, yet not crushed; we are perplexed, but not in despair; persecuted, but not forsaken; struck down, but not destroyed—always carrying about in the body the dying of the Lord Jesus, that the life of Jesus also may be manifested in our body. For we who live are always delivered to death for Jesus' sake, that the life of Jesus also may be manifested in our mortal flesh. . . . Therefore we do not lose heart. Even though our outward man is perishing, yet the inward man is being renewed day by day. For our light affliction, which is but for a moment, is working for us a far more exceeding and eternal weight of glory, while we do not look at the things which are seen, but at the things which are not seen. For the things which are seen are temporary, but the things which are not seen are eternal (II Corinthians 4:8-11, 16-18).

Notice that Paul did not deny his pain. He admitted being hard pressed, perplexed, persecuted, and struck down. At the same time, he was not crushed, in despair, forsaken, or destroyed. Because he was a person of faith, there was a limit to what his suffering could do to him. He saw his suffering as "carrying about in the body the dying of the Lord Jesus." This was necessary for the life of Jesus to be manifested in his body. What this seems to mean is that Paul's suffering was a result of his identification with Jesus Christ in His death. Jesus did say, after all, "If anyone desires to come after Me, let him deny himself, and take up his cross daily, and follow Me. For whoever desires to save his life will lose it, but whoever loses his life for

196

My sake will save it. For what profit is it to a man if he gains the whole world, and is himself destroyed or lost?" (Luke 9:23-25).

Paul also saw the inverse relationship between the outward man and the inward man. As the outward man perishes, the inward man is renewed. Although Paul's suffering was intense and ongoing, he described it as "light affliction" that was "but for a moment." He could do this because he compared the suffering to the "far more exceeding and eternal weight of glory" his affliction was working out in his life. This works, Paul said, as we refuse to focus on what is visible and focus instead on what is invisible. We must do this because visible things are temporary while invisible things are eternal.

Paul's words beg the question: Is it possible to experience this exceeding and eternal weight of glory without the suffering? Is it possible for the life of Jesus to be manifested in our body if we do not carry about in our body the dying of the Lord Jesus? The apparent answer to both questions is no. If we wish to experience the life of Jesus, if we wish to experience the glory, we must embrace the suffering. This does not mean we earn our salvation by suffering; it means if we are genuinely like Christ, we will encounter the suffering that comes to those who identify with Him. Jesus explained this in John 15:19-21.

If you were of the world, the world would love its own. Yet because you are not of the world, but I chose you out of the world, therefore the world hates you. Remember the word that I said to you, 'A servant is not greater than his master.' If they persecuted Me, they will also persecute you. If they kept My word, they will keep yours also. But all these things they will do to you for My name's sake, because they do not know Him who sent Me.

197

Paul had still more to say about his experiences of suffering. As you read his words, think about your own situation. How does it compare to Paul's?

> In all things we commend ourselves as ministers of God: in much patience, in tribulations, in needs, in distresses, in stripes, in imprisonments, in tumults, in labors, in sleeplessness, in fastings; by purity, by knowledge, by longsuffering, by kindness, by the Holy Spirit, by sincere love, by the word of truth, by the power of God, by the armor of righteousness on the right hand and on the left, by honor and dishonor, by evil report and good report; as deceivers, and yet true; as unknown, and yet well known; as dying, and behold we live; as chastened, and yet not killed; as sorrowful, yet always rejoicing; as poor, yet making many rich; as having nothing, and yet possessing all things (II Corinthians 6:4-10).

Notice how Paul intertwines what we might consider the good and the bad. He doesn't divide life into compartments. He views life as one integrated, interrelated whole. On the one hand, Paul refers to his patience, tribulation, needs, distresses, stripes, imprisonments, tumults, labors, sleeplessness, fasting, dishonor, evil report, the rumor that he was a deceiver, the fact that he was unknown, death, chastening, sorrow, and want. On the other hand, his life was characterized by purity, knowledge, longsuffering, kindness, the Holy Spirit, love, the word of truth, honor, good report, and the fact that he was true, well-known, living, rejoicing, making many rich, and possessing all things. Would it have been possible for him to experience the latter without the former? Apparently not. For Paul, everything he experienced in life served to make him what he was.

We have considered the last six verses of Hebrews 11 in previous chapters. These verses set forth the painful experiences of many people of faith who were not spared suffering. They experienced torture, mocking, scourging, chains, imprisonment, stoning, cruel death, temptations, homelessness, destitution, affliction, and torment. But what we have not considered is that although the previous verses in Hebrews 11 may seem to present a brighter story because of the great victories won by people of faith like Moses, Hebrews 11 is not the story of some people of faith who suffered and some who did not. No hero of faith has ever been a stranger to suffering. Instead, Hebrews 11 is the story of some heroes of faith who suffered without relief in this world and others who suffered in the midst of miracles.

Think of the following heroes of faith who are listed in the earlier part of the chapter. Although Abel offered by faith an excellent sacrifice to God, he was murdered by his own brother. Although Noah built an ark by faith for the saving of his family, he was mocked and ridiculed. Although Abraham was the father of all who believe, his wife was kidnapped, he was forsaken by his nephew Lot even though he had befriended Lot, and he had to wait until he was a hundred years old before his promised son Isaac was born. Then the tension between Ishmael and Isaac was so great he had to send Hagar and Ishmael away, and he was tested when God required him to offer Isaac as a sacrifice to God. Although Moses was used of God to bring great deliverance to the people of Israel, he had to choose to "suffer affliction with the people of God . . . esteeming the reproach of Christ greater riches than the treasures in Egypt" (Hebrews 11:25). Therefore, one of the lessons we learn from Hebrews 11 is that even the kind of faith that results in miracles does not exempt us from suffering.

We have also learned that suffering comes at us from a variety of sources. First, some experiences occur when we're rejected by people who do not share our faith, even people we love. Second, we may suffer as a consequence of other people's bad decisions. Third, suffering may result from accidents. In cases like this, there is no intentionality involved, either by us, by other people, or even by God. Fourth, Job's story reveals it is possible that suffering results from a decision God makes without consulting with us or telling us the reason. In such a case, however, James assures that God is merciful and compassionate. For Job, God restored everything he had lost and gave him more besides. Fifth, the Bible includes the account of Paul suffering by the will of God in order to accomplish some desired result in his life. In Paul's case, it was to prevent him from becoming proud and arrogant due to the abundance of revelations he had received. Sixth, some suffering may be due to sickness God has not yet chosen to heal. An example of this would be Timothy's ongoing bout with digestive problems. No doubt Paul had prayed for Timothy's healing, but he gave Timothy a medicinal prescription, perhaps at the suggestion of the physician Luke, Paul's traveling companion. Paul wrote, "No longer drink only water, but use a little wine for your stomach's sake and your frequent infirmities" (I Timothy 5:23).

I am suggesting in this closing chapter that we consider embracing suffering as a friend. Why would we want to do this? First, we should do this because God uses suffering to develop character in those who respond to suffering by trusting in Him. This alone would be sufficient reason. Second, suffering helps us develop empathy for others. Paul said God "comforts us in all our tribulation, that we may be able to comfort those who are in any trouble, with the comfort with which we ourselves are comforted by God. For as the sufferings of Christ abound in us, so our consolation also abounds through Christ" (II Corinthians 1:4-5). We should, Paul wrote, "rejoice with those who rejoice, and weep with those who weep" (Romans 12:15). Third, we should embrace suffering as a friend because suffering lessens our tendency to pass judgment on others. When we have been there, we realize solutions are not quite as simple as they may seem to those who have not suffered. James wrote, "For judgment is without mercy to the one who has shown no mercy. Mercy triumphs over judgment" (James 2:13). Fourth, suffering drives us to seek help from others rather than to indulge in our self-sufficient attitude that we can handle our problems alone. Solomon wrote, "Two are better than one, because they have a good reward for their labor. For if they fall, one will lift up his companion. But woe to him who is alone when he falls, for he has no one to help him up" (Ecclesiastes 4:9-10). Fifth, suffering is to be embraced because it can help us develop humility, which is God's requirement for exaltation. According to James, we should humble ourselves in the sight of the Lord. If we do, He will lift us up.[143] Sixth, we should embrace suffering because it gives us an opportunity to trust God not just in good times, but also in bad. This is when our witness for Christ is most authentic and believable. Seventh, suffering can be our friend because, as Paul discovered, God's strength is made perfect in our weakness.

I admit it seems counterintuitive to us from our twenty-first-century Western mindset, but the Bible tells us we should glory in weakness, rejoice in tribulation, and count it all joy when we experience various trials. This may require us to rethink what the Christian life is all about. It's not about joy versus sorrow, but joy in sorrow. It's not about peace versus turmoil, but peace in the midst of turmoil. It's not about contentment versus need, but contentment in the midst of need. Paul discovered this and explained, "I have learned in whatever state I am, to be content: I know how to be abased, and I know how to abound. Everywhere and in all things I have learned both to be full and to be hungry, both to abound and to suffer need. I can do all things through Christ who strengthens me" (Philippians 4:11-13).

Some things are more important than living a pain-free life—being conformed to the character of Christ and embracing eternity's values. Still, we want to learn our lesson, put pain behind us, and get on with life. But there is always another lesson to learn, and the pain will not go away until sin's final sting—death—is conquered in the resurrection.

The words of C. S. Lewis bear hearing again: "Pain insists upon being tended to. God whispers to us in our pleasures, speaks to us in our conscience, but shouts in our pain: it is His megaphone to rouse a deaf world."[144]

We don't face tests only because God needs to learn about us. We face tests because we need to learn about us. Trials of faith show our hidden weaknesses, and they give us opportunities for unexpected growth—growth that will ultimately result in sharing in Christ's glory.

Think about it: if you embrace suffering as a friend, it is no longer your enemy.

Epilogue

Judy's Story

Many are the opinions as to why God's people suffer. But suffering is a reality, even for believers. Not all of life's trials are handed out the same way to each person. If you talk to enough people, you will find a variety of experiences. But all suffer. Some silently. Some share their pain.

In the more than forty-five years Dan and I have been married, we've had our share of life's trials. When first in the depths of overwhelming trauma, it has seemed God was far away. But we have discovered He walks beside us as we hurt.

After my husband wrote this book about the problem of suffering, but before it was published, we confronted another dimension of suffering we have been dealing with together. Cancer. Cancer is a disease that can strike any part of the human body. One radiologist told me that no part of the body is immune. I've known many who fought and won over this sickness, but many have not.

As we share our experience, you may gain another perspective on why Christians suffer. The Garden of Eden has a lot to do with it, and as much as we would like to change what Adam and Eve did, we can't.

It was cool, but spring was on the way and all was well. We had made plans for an extended trip to California to see our son and daughter and their children. We were to drive into Oregon and have services with Gary and Linda Gleason in Oregon City. Dan was also planning to participate in a theological symposium.

I'd been coughing a lot for several weeks, but that was not unusual for me. Every few years I would contract a bronchial infection and the cough would last for weeks. About the first part of March, I began to notice that my left breast was making some strange changes. It began to turn pinkish and developed an unusual denseness. I thought maybe all the coughing had caused an infection in my chest. Several days later that breast began to feel warm and feverish. My husband prayed for me several times, but there was no change. I knew something wasn't right, so I called my primary doctor's office and told the receptionist I thought my case was an emergency. She talked to the doctor and called me back with an appointment at the end of that day.

The doctor examined me and immediately told me she was setting up an appointment for me to see a cancer specialist. Cancer? Me? This was Friday. Daylight Savings Time was to begin that weekend, but because of thinking so much on this situation, we forgot to turn our clocks forward and were late for church on Sunday.

Monday began a series of tests and doctor visits. Wednesday was my appointment with the cancer specialist. She looked at me before she did the biopsies and told me it looked like inflammatory cancer. I had never heard of it. She said she knew many people who lived long lives after the treatments and surgery. I would lose my left breast if her diagnosis was correct. She walked up to the table in front of me and put her hands on my shoulders, and I could feel her care and concern. A peace settled over me, and I could not believe my response. It was like God was in the room.

I told her, "I believe in miracles and I know I could be healed. But if God chooses for me to go through this, He can guide you and help you know what to do."

When I dressed and left the examination room, I motioned for my husband to come into the open area just behind the waiting room.

I looked in Dan's eyes and felt no panic at all. "She says it is probably inflammatory cancer. She may have to do surgery. The test results may be ready tomorrow."

As long as I live, his response will be nestled in my heart. He didn't say anything. His eyes filled with great drops of water that almost spilled over onto his face. I hugged him and told him everything would be all right. It was then that I realized how much he really did love me. Cancer could mean losing someone. He wanted me to stay with him. He would now put into practice another part of our wedding vows. He had loved me in health; now he would love me in sickness.

It was already settled in my heart. If it was my time to die, I had been granted a wonderful life on this earth. Even with some of its harshness, life had been good to me. Having a wonderful husband and the privilege to do and see so many things gave me thankfulness. Children and grandchildren were added blessings. Being in the ministry all our married life gave us myriad experiences and brought us many friends. Peace seemed to cover me like a warm blanket. I was not afraid.

Dr. James called the next morning. "The tests results are in. It is what I suspected: inflammatory cancer. I have set you up to see an oncologist immediately." My world was about to change drastically. I was about to see if my lifetime of faith would carry me.

During my daily Bible reading, I began to jot down anything that seemed to apply to my situation. The first Scripture was Psalm 33:22: "Let thy mercy, O Lord, be upon us according as we hope in thee." Even if I didn't get through this, I held on to a hope of life eternal.

After mammograms, an MRI, a PET scan, blood work, a sonar heart exam, and various consultations with doctors, I was set up to have a port-a-cath installed in my chest. This would feed the chemical agents into my body and, we hoped, stop the spread of the aggressive inflammatory cancer. The surgeon gave me a few days before the outpatient procedure and told us we could fly to California for a brief trip to see our family. We left on Sunday and returned Wednesday. It wasn't long, but we got to see everyone. My oldest granddaughter was now expecting our first great-grandchild. We saw her carrying the baby boy, and that was worth the trip.

We drove to the hospital early on Friday and got set up for the surgery. I had looked at pictures of the port and was a bit uneasy about having a plastic article with a tube inserted into a vein. It reminded me of a miniature old-time toy top. I survived and was sore for a few days. Early the next week the chemotherapy began. It was my sixty-third birthday, March 31, and I sat in the room where others were getting treatments. The nurse inserted a needle into the port, took a blood test from it, then attached another tube that would feed different types of medicines into my bloodstream. The chemicals would begin to attack the cancer cells. The nurses were cheerful. There was a nice flower garden to look at through the large window if you were blessed to get the right reclining chair. This series of eight treatments would last for sixteen weeks with one treatment every other week.

I finished the first one and felt pretty good after it was over. It didn't seem so bad. Little did I know what was coming.

My husband was scheduled to speak the following week-end in Arkansas, so we decided I would ride along and rest in the motel until he was finished. We would then drive home and enjoy each other's company. But after a few days, my body began to feel weak, and it seemed I could barely function. By the time we left Arkansas for the drive home, I was so weak I couldn't even pull open a door. I was miserable during our drive of more than four hundred miles. It was wonderful to see our house and just crawl into bed.

This started a basic routine of bed rest. This woman who was always doing and going had to make a lifestyle change. "Lord, You will have to help me. I can't do this unless you carry me." My energy level was extremely low. We kept up most of the things around the house together. My husband carried things for me. He vacuumed. I would slowly dust and wipe off the bathroom fixtures.

For four months, I would feel somewhat well for a day or two every two weeks.

Fourteen days after I began my chemotherapy, my hair began to turn loose. In a couple of days, my head was completely pink. It was hard for me to lose the hair I'd always considered to be my glory. Tears filled my eyes as I realized it would have to grow out from the start again. Even as a baby, I was born with lots of dark, curly hair. Now I joined other ladies being treated with chemotherapy.

Our church, The Sanctuary, took up a collection for me to buy a wig or hats. That was so special to me. The cards were beautiful, and the donations inside made me cry. I learned to wear baseball hats, turbans, scarves, hats, and wigs. I just could not show my pink head. I really knew now why the Bible classified a woman's long hair as her glory.

I was changed outwardly, but my heart was set on the Lord who sustained me. He became very near and dear to me as I learned to put complete trust in Him.

After the chemotherapy treatments ended, I waited about a month to build up strength, and then it was time for the surgery. August fifth arrived. The radical mastectomy did not hurt so much, but the fact that a part of me was missing did. The surgery healed as expected. It was a long and arduous time of bandages, drains, and rest.

The first time I looked at myself with the bruises and eight-inch scar across my chest, I almost panicked. Then I realized how truly blessed I was to have found the cancer quickly before it spread into the body. The doctor told me on one office visit that it looked as bad as it would ever look. It would get better. Slowly, I got used to the appearance and began to look at the scar as a badge of courage. I wanted to survive.

I had already received many cards, letters, emails, phone calls, and packages from my friends and relatives. People from all over were praying for me. I took this knowledge and held on to it. There were also prayer cloths in my pillow from several acquaintances or churches.

I was scheduled to meet with the surgeon a week after the surgery. My husband and I waited in one of the rooms, anxious to hear what the results would be after they tested the tissues and lymph nodes.

The surgeon came in, and her face gave it away. There was a satisfied glow that came from her smile. She looked at us and said, "The pathologist's report says there is no residual cancer in the tissue. Only one lymph node was affected by the cancer, and it is dead." Dan and I both started to cry. I hadn't cried over the cancer since it was diagnosed. It seemed that I knew God would do what was best for me. If He chose to take me, I would be a winner. If He chose to let me have more years, I would also be a winner. I knew I was in God's hands. My entire life from a child had been lived for the day when I would be in Heaven with the Lord. As they say, though, "Everyone wants to go to Heaven, but nobody wants to die." This was where I seemed to be standing. My hope of life was increased a hundredfold.

The next step would be six and a half weeks of radiation to be sure there were no surviving cancer cells on the outer skin. The treatments were five days a week, every week, and each one was a long process since it took awhile to position me just right on the table under the machine. Then it was another ten minutes of lying perfectly still.

During the actual treatment, I would pray and ask God to help me endure. Then I would pray for myself and others in my life. Usually this was done to pop tunes or rock songs playing over the speakers in the room. Now that is some unusual background music for prayer! But I learned to shut it out and barely notice it.

I edged toward the final week where the treatment would be only about twenty seconds once they had me situated. That was a relief from the previous long treatments.

The doctor seemed to think I would be clear to go when all was said and done. I would have to visit different doctors so they could keep an eye on me through the years. I have thanked God many times for the doctors and technicians who have worked so hard to learn what to do when life throws those unexpected curves. I told each of them that I knew God could guide them to do what I needed. He was with me and would help me and them.

One of the greatest things that happened to me during this ordeal was after the chemotherapy ended. I had given the six nurses a copy of my book 65 Short Stories and wrote a note to each of them in the front. I had always wanted my life to count and my light to shine in the world. The ladies sent me a card, and all signed it except for one of them. She was off work, so she sent me a card on her own. I broke down and cried when it came. She wrote: *Dear Judy, Thank you so much for the book of your personal stories. I will treasure it! You were such an*

209

inspiration during this part of your treatment. You are truly a testimony of Jesus' attributes!

For years and years I had prayed to be a light to others and to live like our Lord. I had to face such a tragic part of life to hear this from someone I had not even known. In my suffering, someone saw Jesus in my life as I leaned on Him and kept my attitude on higher things.

Suffering comes in many different ways to every individual. No matter how low or how severe the trial is, God will not change. He will be there. We may not always get what we want, but we can be sure He is still in control.

I don't know what the future holds, but whatever comes, I am counting on my Lord to do the right thing in my life.

Daniel's Story

When I wrote the manuscript for this book, I had no idea what the future held for Judy and me. I submitted the manuscript to Robin Johnston, editor in chief of the United Pentecostal Church International, on January 6, 2009. On March 13, 2009, Judy was diagnosed with inflammatory breast cancer.

Judy and I were quickly thrust onto a path we never thought we would follow. We experienced a sharp learning curve about a subject we had never previously considered. We discovered that inflammatory cancer is aggressive and fast growing. On March 31, Judy's sixty-third birthday, she had her first chemotherapy treatment. These treatments continued for sixteen weeks. On August 5, Judy endured a radical mastectomy. When she had regained some of her strength from this, she embarked on a daily schedule (Monday-Friday) of radiation for six and a half weeks.

On December 14, Judy had an appointment with her oncologist for a follow-up visit. She said, "I've been waiting to see you to fill out my Christmas greeting. What should I put in it?" He said, "You can tell them you are cancer free, you're in remission, you're well."

Between the diagnosis, "You have inflammatory breast cancer," and the marvelous words, "cancer free," Judy was an astounding example of deep faith in God, the joy of the Lord as her strength, and peace that passes understanding. She was never depressed or in despair. She wasted no time with questions like "Why did God let this happen?" or "What did I do to deserve this?" All of this was in spite of the fact that Judy experienced continuous suffering.

Because of the aggressive nature of inflammatory cancer, she was treated with strong doses of chemotherapy.

During those sixteen weeks, she spent most of her time in bed, exhausted. Her beautiful long hair fell out, leaving her completely bald. Most foods, including those she had always enjoyed, repulsed her. She could no longer cook those tasty meals I had enjoyed for forty-five years. I learned what it meant to eat frozen dinners prepared by me in the microwave. I also discovered that not all frozen dinners are created equal. Judy lost thirty-five pounds.

I feel so blessed to have a wife who does not just theorize about faith and trust in God, but who lives a life characterized by these virtues. She believes God will do what is right for her. She does not think we can manipulate God to make Him do what we think best. Although Judy enjoys life and wanted to live many more years, including long enough to see our first great-grandson, who was born on June 10 in California, she was willing to depart and be with Christ if that was the will of God.

We learned the importance of talking with other people who had been down this path. We've always believed that openness is better than secrecy, and that belief was confirmed during Judy's trial. She was often encouraged by talking with other women who had experienced breast cancer. She saw again, as we had seen during previous seasons of suffering, the truth of the adage, "Joy shared is a joy doubled; a sorrow shared is a sorrow halved."

Firsthand, we learned the value of being supported by the prayers of people of faith. This was not a figment of our imagination. In an almost tangible way, we could sense the strength and hope that sustained us as a result of the prayers of our brothers and sisters in Christ.

One of Judy's greatest challenges, the moment she was most severely tested, was when she first saw the scar left by her surgery. Even then, however, she found strength in the support of a friend who had been where she was. But for about four months, Judy did not want me to see the scar. Finally, during an early December trip to see our great-grandson, she allowed me to look at the wound. To me, it is her badge of courage. She is a strong, courageous woman. Her strength comes from her trust in God, her healthy relationship with God, and her connections with those who share her faith.

If I had known before I submitted this book manuscript what I know now, would I change anything?

No.

The understanding of the role of suffering in a believer's life that is presented in this book is biblical, not theoretical. Since it is biblical, it is true and practical.

I recently read the words of John Piper, a minister who faced his own battle with cancer. His words resonated with me. "Cancer does not win if you die. It wins if you fail to cherish Christ. God's design is to wean you off the breast of the world and feast you on the sufficiency of Christ."[145]

Here are some other words—inspired words—that resonate with me. When Paul unsuccessfully pleaded three times with the Lord for the removal of the messenger of Satan that was buffeting him, the Lord said, "My grace is sufficient for you, for My strength is made perfect in weakness." Paul, a man of profound faith, then wrote these immortal words: "Therefore most gladly I will rather boast in my infirmities, that the power of Christ may rest upon me. Therefore I take pleasure in infirmities, in reproaches, in needs, in persecutions, in distresses, for Christ's sake. For when I am weak, then I am strong" (II Corinthians 12:9-10).

Although Judy's experience produced physical weakness, both of us feel stronger in our faith as a result of this period of suffering. We have seen firsthand how God sustains, strengthens, and encourages even in the midst of pain and uncertainty.

We have learned, as did Job, that we need God more than we need answers.

Endnotes

[1] See Isaiah 2:1-4.

[2] Genesis 1:26-27.

[3] Genesis 1:28. When God commanded Adam and Eve to subdue the earth, they had not yet sinned and no curse had been placed on creation. It is interesting that after the introduction of sin and the curse on the earth, God gave Noah a commission similar to that given to Adam and Eve, but Noah's commission did not include "subduing" the earth. (See Genesis 9:1-7.) After the introduction of sin, human beings could no longer subdue the earth. This is vividly witnessed in every storm, flood, and earthquake.

[4] Genesis 2:25; 3:7.

[5] Genesis 3:8-12.

[6] Genesis 3:14-15.

[7] Genesis 3:16.

[8] Genesis 3:17-19.

[9] Genesis 3:22-24.

[10] Genesis 6:8.

[11] I Peter 2:23.

[12] The righteous are not the only ones who suffer in this life. "The way of the unfaithful is hard" (Proverbs 13:15).

[13] "Abimelech" (Hebrew, "my father is king") was a dynastic title used of many kings.

[14] Hebrews 11:33.

[15] David Hume, Dialogues concerning Natural Religion, in John G. Stackhouse Jr., Can God Be Trusted? (New York: Oxford University Press, 1998), 11.

[16] Ephesians 1:5, 9, 11.

[17] Genesis 21:33.

[18] Exodus 3:14.

[19] Clark Pinnock, et al., The Openness of God: A Biblical Challenge to the Traditional Understanding of God (Downers Grove, IL: InterVarsity Press, 1994), 121.

[20] Acts 2:23; Romans 8:29; 11:2; I Peter 1:2.

[21] We must also consider what it means to be human. If we were incapable of suffering, would we still be human?

[22] Daniel 4:17, 25, 32; 5:21; Romans 13:1.

[23] See also Hebrews 12:2.

[24] The imprecatory psalms are those in which the author invokes divine judgment on the enemies of Israel and of God. They include Psalms 7, 35, 40, 55, 58, 59, 69, 79, 109, 137, 139, 144. Some of these psalms also fall within the category of the psalms of lament. Psalms of individual lament include 3-7, 12, 13, 22, 25-28, 35, 38-40, 42, 43, 51, 54-57, 59, 61, 63, 64, 69-71, 86, 88, 102, 109, 120, 130, 140-143. Psalms of national lament include 44, 60, 74, 79, 80, 83, 85, 90, 123.

[25] Romans 8:35-39.

[26] Romans 8:28-29.

[27] Acts 10:34.

[28] Matthew 11:20-24.

[29] I Kings 22:19-23; II Kings 6:19; Psalm 18:25-26.

[30] The sentiments expressed in this song describe the kinds of experiences that cause us to question. "We'll Understand It Better," by C. A. Tindley, and arranged by F. A. Clark, published by the Gospel Publishing House, 1957, number 96.

[31] Some may think of Paul's words in I Corinthians 13:12 as a promise that we will one day understand all things: "For now we see in a mirror, dimly, but then face to face. Now I know in part, but then I shall know just as I also am known." However, the context has to do with the exercise of spiritual gifts, not with suffering. (See Daniel L. Segraves, "That Which Is Perfect [I Corinthians 13:10]: A Non-Eschatological Approach" [MA thesis, Western Seminary, 1993].)

[32] I Peter 1:16.

[33] Leviticus 11:41-47.

[34] I Peter 1:14-15.

[35] John 4:24; Colossians 1:15; I Timothy 1:17; Hebrews 11:27; Jeremiah 23:23-24.

[36] Some have thought God had a body prior to the Incarnation, known perhaps as the Word, and that this body in some way was transformed into the human body of Jesus. The rationale for this is that there must have been a visible body before the Incarnation in order for angels (as in Job 1:6; 2:1) or humans (Isaiah 6:1) to see Him. Since Jesus was "in the form of God" (Philippians 2:6) prior to the Incarnation, some think this means God had a permanent visible body of some kind. But the Bible asserts that God is invisible. (See John 1:18; 6:46; I Timothy 1:17; I John 4:12; Exodus 33:20.) The various appearances of God in the Old Testament are examples of what are commonly called "theophanies." These are temporary and varied manifestations of God. God was manifested at various times as

a cloud, a pillar of fire, an angel, thunder and lightning, and a whirlwind. Many of the appearances of God are visions. It is the nature of a vision (or a dream) that what is being seen is a representation of reality, not reality itself. Passages describing something taking place in the realm of the spirit—like encounters between God and angels—should be understood as representing what is unique to the spiritual realm that is invisible to the natural eye. Our understanding of how spirit beings interact with each other is limited by the fact that we presently are incapable of entering directly into the spiritual realm. All descriptions of interaction between spirit beings in Scripture are accommodated to human understanding and to the limitations of human language, as are descriptions of God as having eyes, hands, nostrils, feet, wings, or a back. Reality is represented by these terms, but the terms themselves are metaphorical. The word translated "form," in the description of Jesus as eternally existing in the "form" of God is morphē, a word that emphasizes the essence of something. The NIV translation is helpful here: "Who, being in very nature God . . ." Before the Incarnation, Jesus eternally existed as God, but this does not mean He had a permanent, visible form that looked like a human being. (See Hebrews 10:5.)

[37] Here are two current ideas about the image of God in man: (1) Some ideas emphasize the fact that man (i.e., mankind) was created male and female, thus in relationship. This view holds that the image of God is seen in the idea of relationship itself (i.e., God in some way experiences inner-relationships within Himself). (2) Others, based on the practice of ancient emperors of placing statues of themselves in remote parts of their empires to mark off those areas as being under the emperors' authority, suggest that God placed humans on earth as a kind of symbol of His authority on earth. But the first view fails to account for the fact that, according to Genesis 2:7, Adam was created before Eve. We don't know how much time elapsed before Eve was created, but we do know that during this time when Adam existed alone, God put him in the Garden of Eden and gave him responsibilities. During this time, Adam named "every beast of the field and every bird of the air" (Genesis 2:19). Was not Adam already in the image of God when he existed alone? Paul wrote, "For a man indeed ought not to cover his head, since he is the image and glory of God; but woman is the glory of man" (I Corinthians 11:7). Although Paul did not deny that the woman was also the image of God, he specifically described the male as being "the image of God." If the image of God is essentially seen in relationship, it is difficult to see how Adam could have been in the image of God before Eve was created or how Paul could accurately say that a male is the image

of God. Further, language similar to that of Genesis 1:26-27 appears in Genesis 5:3, which declares that "Adam . . . begot a son in his own likeness, after his image, and named him Seth." If the image of God in Adam required Adam to exist in relationship with Eve, it is difficult to see how Adam's essential image could be reproduced in Seth, a lone male. Indeed, in this view, no human, isolated for whatever reason from others, could be truly said to be in the image of God. The problem with the second view above is that it is anachronistic. The ancient rulers who placed statues of themselves at the remote corners of their kingdoms did not exist at the time humans were created. God did not pattern His creation of humans after a practice that would arise among pagan emperors many years later.

[38] Perhaps it is not completely appropriate to think of God as a "being," since we usually connect the idea of "being" with creation. But language sometimes fails us when we speak of God.

[39] Genesis 2:19.

[40] See I Corinthians 2:11; Romans 8:16.

[41] See Hebrews 4:12; I Thessalonians 5:23; Luke 1:46-47. For a discussion of the relationship between the human soul and spirit, see the comments on Hebrews 4:12 in Daniel L. Segraves, Hebrews: Better Things, Vol. 1 (Hazelwood, MO: Word Aflame Press, 1996), 122-128.

[42] II Corinthians 4:4.

[43] Ephesians 1:18.

[44] See, e.g., Numbers 16:6-7; 17:5; Deuteronomy 7:6-7.

[45] Genesis 3:6.

[46] See Deuteronomy 30:19.

[47] See Joshua 24:15.

[48] See II Samuel 24:10-15.

[49] Proverbs 1:29.

[50] Romans 5:12.

[51] Romans 3:23.

[52] See also Romans 3:13-18; 7:15-24.

[53] The KJV translates the last phrase "from the evil," but the presence of the definite article before the word "evil" suggests a specific evil, recognized in more recent translations as the "evil one," Satan.

[54] John 8:32.

[55] Jesus is the image of God in a unique way not shared by other humans. By means of the virgin conception (He had no human father; God was His Father in a very real sense), He is not merely the image of God as it pertains to His humanity, but as it pertains to His deity. (See Hebrews 1:3;

II Corinthians 4:4; Colossians 1:15.) Since deity is unique and cannot be duplicated or created, this means that Jesus is Himself God. (See Isaiah 43:10.)

[56] See also II Corinthians 7:4; I Thessalonians 4:18; Psalm 119:50, 75-76.

[57] Philippians 4:8.

[58] Philippians 4:9.

[59] Leviticus 19:17.

[60] Deuteronomy 19:11.

[61] Deuteronomy 22:13.

[62] I Kings 22:8.

[63] Amos 5:15.

[64] Psalm 97:10.

[65] Psalm 101:3.

[66] Psalm 119:104.

[67] Psalm 119:113.

[68] Psalm 119:163.

[69] Proverbs 6:16-19.

[70] Proverbs 8:36.

[71] II Corinthians 12:9.

[72] See I Thessalonians 4:13, 18.

[73] Some of the insights in this chapter are taken from an unpublished paper by Gerry Breshears, PhD, "A Practical Strategy for Ministering to the Suffering." Breshears is professor of theology at Western Seminary, Portland, OR.

[74] Matthew 26:36-45.

[75] John H. Sailhamer, NIV Compact Bible Commentary (Grand Rapids: Zondervan Publishing House, 1994), 322.

[76] Psalm 132:11.

[77] Psalm 37:10, 12, 14, 16, 17, 20, 21, 28, 32, 34, 35, 38, 40.

[78] Psalm 37:6, 12, 16, 17, 21, 25, 29, 30, 32, 37.

[79] Psalm 37:1, 2, 9, 13, 15, 22, 36.

[80] Psalm 37:3-5, 7-9, 11, 14, 18, 19, 22-24, 26-28, 31, 33-34, 37, 40.

[81] Psalm 37:16-17, 21, 32.

[82] Psalm 37:14, 28, 34, 40.

[83] Earl D. Radmacher, ed., The Nelson Study Bible, New King James Version (Nashville, TN: Thomas Nelson Publishers, 1997), 914.

[84] Matthew 5:5.

[85] Compare with Psalm 2:4.

[86] Compare with Psalm 1:6.

219

[87] Psalm 36:12.

[88] See also Psalm 37:3, 9, 11.

[89] See also Psalm 37:6.

[90] Compare with Psalm 37:3, 9, 11, 27.

[91] Compare with Psalm 1:2.

[92] With some revision, these comments on Psalm 37 are taken from Daniel L. Segraves, The Messiah in the Psalms: Discovering Christ in Unexpected Places (Hazelwood, MO: Word Aflame Press, 2007), 126-132.

[93] Daniel L. Segraves, James: Faith At Work (Hazelwood, MO: Word Aflame Press, 1995), 190-191.

[94] The American College Dictionary (C. L. Barnhart, Editor in Chief; New York: Random House, 1964), s.v., "chance."

[95] William Sanford LaSor, et al., Old Testament Survey (Grand Rapids, MI: Eerdmans Publishing Co., 1982), 533-34.

[96] LaSor, Old Testament Survey, 534.

[97] Proverbs 1:4.

[98] Proverbs 1: 8.

[99] This discussion on Proverbs 22:6 is adapted from Daniel L. Segraves, Ancient Wisdom for Today's World: Proverbs (Hazelwood, MO: Word Aflame Press, 1990), 232-34.

[100] Ibid., 583.

[101] Ecclesiastes 12:1, 13-14.

[102] This comparison of Job, Proverbs, and Ecclesiastes is adapted from Daniel L. Segraves, Ancient Wisdom for Today's World: Proverbs (Hazelwood, MO: Word Aflame Press, 1990), 349-352.

[103] See also Ezekiel 14:20.

[104] C. S. Lewis, The Problem of Pain (New York: HarperOne, 2001), 91.

[105] Job 2:11-13.

[106] See James and Marti Hefley, By Their Blood: Christian Martyrs of the Twentieth Century, 2nd ed. (Grand Rapids, MI: Baker Book House, 1996). Much of this chapter is adapted from Daniel L. Segraves, First Peter: Standing Fast in the Grace of God (Hazelwood, MO: Word Aflame Press, 1999).

[107] See T. F. Tenney, "Persecution Fires in 1996," Pentecostal Herald, September 1996:5-6.

[108] Revelation 20:10.

[109] Mark 16:17.

[110] James 4:7.

[111] John 7:3-5.

112 Mark 3:21.

113 Mark 3:22.

114 James 1:3-4.

115 Craig S. Keener, The Bible Background Commentary, New Testament (Downers Grove, IL: InterVarsity Press, 1993), 642.

116 Keener, The Bible Background Commentary, 642.

117 Keener, The Bible Background Commentary, 642, 719.

118 Wayne Grudem, I Peter; Tyndale New Testament Commentaries (Grand Rapids, MI: William B. Eerdmans, 1988), 124.

119 Keener, The Bible Background Commentary, 643.

120 I Corinthians 7:21-23.

121 Keener, The Bible Background Commentary, 643.

122 Deuteronomy 23:15-16.

123 http://arthritis.about.com/b/2007/08/20/the-use-of-painkillers-has-nearly-doubled-in-recent-years.htm. Accessed March 16, 2008.

124 I Peter 3:16.

125 I Peter 3:17.

126 I Peter 3:18; 4:1.

127 I Peter 4:5.

128 Walter Bauer, A Greek-English Lexicon of the New Testament and Other Early Christian Literature (trans. William F. Arndt and F. Wilbur Gingrich; Rev. F. Wilbur Gingrich and Frederick W. Danker, 2nd ed.; Chicago: University of Chicago Press, 1979), 486.

129 Matthew 5:12.

130 Keener, The Bible Background Commentary, 718.

131 Keener, The Bible Background Commentary, 720.

132 Acts 11:26.

133 Acts 26:28.

134 http://www.cmds.org/Ethics/2_6.htm. Accessed May 20, 1999.

135 Isaiah 66:22.

136 Psalm 22:7-8.

137 Hebrews 2:12.

138 II Corinthians 11:23-27.

139 http://www.christianitytoday.com/ct/article_print.html?id=54424. Accessed March 21, 2008.

140 Job 23:10.

141 Romans 8:28.

142 Revelation 7:17.

143 James 4:10.

[144] C. S. Lewis, The Problem of Pain, 91.

[145] http://www.christianitytoday.com/ct/2009/decemberweb-only/151-11.0.html?start=2. Accessed December 16, 2009.